TRADITIONAL BRAZILIAN BLACK MAGIC

TRADITIONAL BRAZILIAN BLACK MAGIC

The Secrets of the Kimbanda Magicians

DIEGO DE OXÓSSI

Destiny Books
Rochester, Vermont

Destiny Books
One Park Street
Rochester, Vermont 05767
www.DestinyBooks.com

Text stock is SFI certified

Destiny Books is a division of Inner Traditions International

Originally published in Portuguese in 2018 under the title *Desvendando Exu: O Guardião dos Caminhos* by Editora Arole Cultural
First U.S. edition published in 2021 by Destiny Books

Cataloging-in-Publication Data for this title is available from the Library of Congress

ISBN 978-1-64411-226-7 (print)
ISBN 978-1-64411-227-4 (ebook)

Printed and bound in the United States by Lake Book Manufacturing, Inc.
The text stock is SFI certified. The Sustainable Forestry Initiative® program promotes sustainable forest management.

10 9 8 7 6 5 4 3 2 1

Text design and layout by Virginia Scott Bowman
This book was typeset in Garamond Premier Pro and Optima with Fnord used as the display typeface

To send correspondence to the author of this book, mail a first-class letter to the author c/o Inner Traditions • Bear & Company, One Park Street, Rochester, VT 05767, and we will forward the communication, or contact the author directly at **talkto@diegodeoxossi.com.br**.

Ô me disseram que a minha Casa ia cair,
People said my Temple was going down,

Mas ela é de madeira que não dá cupim!
But it's made of wood that doesn't get termites!

Foi o Seo 7 que me deu,
It was Mr. Seven Crossroads who gave it to me,

Só ele pode destruir!
So he's the only one who can destroy it!

Nela Exu é Rei e já ganhou coroa,
In my Temple Eshu is crowned King,

A sua gargalhada não é à toa!
That's why he laughs and sings!

Contents

Foreword

JOÃO BATISTA LIBANIO, a Brazilian Jesuit and doctor of theology, says that theology is the science that studies faith—not the faith of others but the theologian's own faith. Therefore, it is almost necessary that the theologian be an experiencer of a religion, and it's this religion that he or she will think about and research. Contrary to what some may think, this area of knowledge is not dedicated just to Christianity. Each religious tradition has its own theology, and this theology is born from the observation of ritual elements, from experiences with the sacred, and from the analysis of sacred stories, songs, and prayers. Theology analyzes all elements of a particular religion, including its history and philosophy, to discover what purpose God has chosen for us through it. For if religion is the form that men have created to approach God, theology is God's way of reaching us, to paraphrase Libanio.

The theology of African-origin traditions, such as Batuque and Candomblé, first arose timidly but is now rising fiercely and has, through the commitment of some Brazilian researchers, gained strength. Intense attacks by fundamentalist segments of society on these religions—classifying them as demonic or primitive in a demonstration of ignorance and racism—have galvanized this interest and research. Believers in and practitioners of these religions have been stimulated to search for knowledge, many daring to enter academia and to graduate with degrees in law, history, sociology, pedagogy, psychology, religion sciences, and philosophy, as well as theology, with the intention of analyzing elements of these African-origin traditions.

We are still a long way from building in the Brazilian state of Rio Grande do Sul, a real school of theology for African-origin religious traditions (or *Afro-theology,* as I have defined it), in the mold of other religious traditions, but we are already offering training courses in this area whose theoretical references are immersed in and guided by Molefi Kete Asante, an African American professor and philosopher, and his book *Afrocentricity.*

The College of Umbanda Theology in São Paulo is the first and only college in Brazil dedicated to non-Christian religions; this school of thought focuses on analyzing African Brazilian religions and contributes much to academia and the understanding of African faiths as a whole. Despite these two initiatives in Rio Grande do Sul and São Paulo, there is still a lack of theological reflection on what we call marginal spirits: *compadres* and *comadres, catiços,* the Eshus and Pombagiras. In this book, Diego de Oxóssi has worked to fill that gap.

I met Diego through Orkut, an online social networking service that no longer exists. It has been more than ten years since he came to my house to consult **Ifá** divination and find out what path he should take in his life. Seeing how far he has progressed, I am glad to know that he followed the advice of **Ọ̀rúnmìlà,** the god of wisdom in Yoruba mythology. Diego brings an academic approach to his subject, with careful research and documented sources, which guarantees that his work is highly reliable. In particular, the way he traces the history of religious practices deserves a highlight. His interpretation of the slavery of the Eshu brings elements perhaps never before considered.

In an unpretentious and didactic way, Diego points out several ways for theological reflection on the Eshus. In the chapter on the relations between the **Òrìsà Eṣu** and the spirit-deity Eshu, the author produces a true Kimbanda theology. Also worthy of note are his reflections on the relationship between Eshu and the Judeo-Christian devil.

In this book you will find precision and thoroughness: the author provides excellent historical-theological material on the Kimbanda tradition. He presents a logical line of thought from history to theology, bringing to light elements not discussed until today, which makes this book a unique contribution to the literature on African Brazilian religions.

Hendrix Silveira
Bàbá Hendrix de Ọ̀rúnmìlà
Bàbálórìṣà at Ilè Àṣe Òrìṣà Wúre

Hendrix Silveira has an M.A. and a Ph.D. in theology from EST College and is a theological adviser to the African-religious People's Council of the State of Rio Grande do Sul, Brazil.

Acknowledgments

TO MY FAMILY AND FRIENDS who accompanied, supported, and often helped me to get here and who, even without sharing the same faith and without understanding the nights awakened by the sound of the drums, always believed with all their hearts when I told them to *trust Eshu.*

To Mãe Ieda do Ogum, my black mother, and to Eshu King of 7 Crossroads, the Legbara Eshu who taught me everything I know about Kimbanda and who took me by the hand and told me *come* when everything else seemed to collapse. As the saying goes, he gave me the porridge and the belt—the good and the bad.

To Eshu 7 Facadas, my *compadre,* my drunken rascal, and my eternal guardian, for everything—for the Kingdom, for the world, for existing in my life!

And, no less important, to my dear friend, teacher, and *babalorixá* Hendrix de Orumilaia, who kindly prefaced the Portuguese edition of the book, fully maintained in this second edition, and who, with his words, gave me the encouragement and courage to follow the paths of the *orishas* to my destiny.

About the African and Portuguese Vocabulary Used in This Book

AFRICAN BRAZILIAN RELIGIONS have been studied and codified by their practitioners for some years now. Fortunately, many of these practitioners have attained academic degrees, until then dominated by a white, Christian elite who did not accept the rise of black people to the chairs of universities. A great effort is being made to qualify the sources of research, and a process of reafricanization of rites and myths has been happening in a unique way that contributes greatly to the preservation and valorization of African culture and its influence on the ethnolinguistic formation of the Brazilian people.

For this reason, words of African origin—mostly Yoruba, Ewe-Fon, and Kimbundu—are given in this book in the original or commonly accepted form used in academic studies that have preceded this work. They are marked in either bold or bold italics as a way of highlighting and encouraging the continued study of these languages, while roman italics are used for Portuguese words and terms created by the author. These African languages are tonal, with differing tones or pitches used to convey meaning. The following list compares the original African terms with the Portuguese variants of most of the African words presented in this book, with definitions and translations of the words provided in parentheses. Emphasized or accented letters are underlined.

African	Portuguese	English
àse	*axé*	*ashé,* a West African philosophical concept, also spiritual strength
bàbá	*babá*	father, also used as an honorific
bàbálórìsà	*babalorixá*	*babalorishá,* a male priest, also used as a title
egun	*almas*	souls
Èsù	*Exu*	Eshu, an ***òrìsà*** in Yoruba religion, referred to both singularly and as a group of ***òrìsàs***
Ìgbàlè	*ibalé* or *bale*	House of Souls, the area in religious temples dedicated to worship of the anonymous dead
ilè	*ilê*	house
Ilé Ibo Akú	*casa dos mortos*	House of the Dead, the area in religious temples dedicated to worshipping the honorable dead from one's religious and genetic family
ìyá	*iá* or *iyá*	mother, also used as an honorific
ìyálórìsà	*iyalorixá*	*ialorishá,* a female priest, also used as a title
ìyàwó	*iaô*	novice or initiate
kalunga	*calunga*	cemetery
mariwô	*mariô*	palm leaves
nganga or ***inyanga***	*ganga*	herbalist, spiritual healer, or priest
ogo	*ogó*	phallus, the magic symbol of Eshu
òrìsà	*orixá*	*orisha,* general Yoruba term for deity, also used as a title or honorific

There are also Portuguese words featured in this book with no African-language equivalent used in Brazil.

Portgueseꟷ	English
aprontado or *pronto*	those who passed by the *aprontamento* rite, considered to be a religious adult
aprontamento	rite of passage
cachaça	distilled spirit made from fermented sugarcane juice
calundu	African-derived religious practices in colonial Brazil, literally meaning "grimace" or "ugly face"
compadre	buddy
curimba	sacred song or prayer for invocation
kimbandeiro	sorcerer
lomba	hill
nação	a unified collection of religious nations re-created by enslaved people in the Americas
omoté	consecrated grave where a spirit is worshipped
pemba	conically shaped limestone chalk
terreira or *terreiro*	African religious temple
zimba	Eshu's magical symbol

INTRODUCTION

When Spirits Come Back to Life

THE MAGICAL PRACTICE AND PERFORMANCE of energy manipulation rituals that seek to honor deities and ask them to interfere and modify the situations around us are present in all spiritual traditions of the world. Even in Western religions such as Catholicism, for example, it is possible to find acts in which the use of natural elements such as plants, water, and food and drink take on magical symbolism and become sacred artifacts in the form of incense, holy water, and the wafer (body) and wine (blood) of Christ.

All these traditions and religions, in addition to deities, honor the spirits of relatives or of people who accomplished outstanding deeds in life with offerings and celebrations in their memory. However, the main difference between African-based religions and other religions is the belief in the capacity of these deities and spirits to temporarily return to life and share their powers and abilities with those who offer them homage. We call this phenomenon *spiritual embodiment* or *possession*.

To those who are just starting to study African-based religions and are unfamiliar with these practices, it is important to say that though the expressions *spiritual embodiment* and *possession* may seem overwhelming or frightening—especially because they bring to mind images created by horror films of spirits and demonic entities who haunt people—in these African traditions, such as Kimbanda, this act is considered sacred.

Above all, its practitioners—called "mediums"—spontaneously and voluntarily accept this spiritual embodiment. It is through these mediums that communion takes place and humans and gods become one.

Whether this embodiment or possession is experienced in secret rites of initiation or in public festivals, it is through this phenomenon that the deities and spirits come back to life and enjoy worldly pleasures again. They receive their offerings in both a symbolic and real way—eating, drinking, singing, dancing, and talking directly with the faithful, bringing to the *real* world what in other traditions and religions is experienced only in a *symbolic* manner.

However, it is necessary to understand the difference between the expressions *spiritual embodiment* and *possession,* since the dynamics by which they are performed are opposite and complementary. For that, it is necessary, first, to understand the difference between the energies worshipped in these religions: *deities* and *spirits.*

Regardless of their ethnic-geographical origin in Africa, as we will see in the next chapters, when enslaved black men and women arrived in the Americas through the diaspora, their spiritual beliefs and practices were adapted and contextualized to the new reality. With this, many rites and customs were lost, and others had to be adapted while maintaining their essence, which, to simplify the understanding, we summarize in two distinct groups.

The first group refers to the worship of primary energies such as fire, water, and earth; the seasons, the phases of the moon, and other natural phenomena; and the powers of life, death, and rebirth. These energies, which are personified and individualized as deities and assume a sacred and divine character, are called *orishas, voduns, inkices,* or *loás.* As deities, they are *supernatural powers with the ability to intervene in human reality, created spontaneously or by another deity, and are eternal and immortal.*

At the same time, practices in Africa are still based on the cult of deceased ancestors and relatives, believing in the perpetuity of the soul after the physical death of matter and honoring these souls in individual and collective memory. These entities—*who may or may not maintain their antemortem individualizations in their postmortem performance and who are characterized, precisely, by the finitude of their existence among mortals*—we call spirits, spiritual entities, or spirit guides. Once we understand the difference between *deities* and *spirits,* we start to understand the difference between the phenomenon of *possession* and *spiritual embodiment.*

Possession is reserved for *deities*—when a deity completely takes over the body and the consciousness of the practitioner who worships it. The individual completely loses his or her earthly individuality and transforms, even if momentarily, into the god or goddess who is manifesting on the physical plane. In this sense, during the initiation rituals of African-based religions, it is said that the deity to which a novice is then dedicated is rooted in his body in a real way, through the rubbing of powders, seeds, and magic elements over the skin or into the bloodstream through scarification. Once the deity is planted and the initiate becomes accustomed to it, he also becomes a part of it, living in a symbiotic relationship. For this reason, the phenomenon of possession is, in some groups, also called *ex-corporation,* which occurs *from the inside out.*

The second phenomenon, called *spiritual embodiment,* is reserved for spiritual entities and occurs *from the outside in.* In this case, the energy that takes on the consciousness—whether completely or partially—of the initiate who invokes it is external, and the coupling of the two, initiate and spiritual entity, forms a third and greater force, as in a mathematical calculation in which the sum of one plus one becomes greater than two. A prayer-song in Kimbanda explains this situation by saying that "everything that is mine [practitioner] is hers [spiritual entity] . . . not everything that is hers, is mine." For this reason, during the phenomenon of spiritual embodiment, the spirit in question can, to a greater or lesser extent, present specific characteristics from when it was alive and still enjoy aspects of the embodied initiate. An example is the knowledge of foreign languages: the embodying spirit can communicate in English, for example, even if in life the spirit only spoke Portuguese—as long as the initiate knows both languages.

The spirits are arranged hierarchically in Traditional Kimbanda, and the main function of the different rituals that compose these hierarchies is to allow the bond and coupling between spirit and initiate to become ever more complete and harmonious so that the spirit can present itself more fully and the consciousness of the initiate is less present during spiritual embodiment. (The spirit hierarchies of Kimbanda are more fully explained in the chapter "Spirit-Deities.") For this reason, it is important to say that no initiate begins his journey with unconscious spiritual embodiment or is authorized to perform rituals in which the real and complete presence of the spirit is necessary. It is for this reason that many temples carry out so-called tests on spiritual entities (such as stepping on fire, eating glass, or swallowing small pieces of cotton in flames): specific rituals that aim to verify how intense and complete the spiritual embodiment is so that, from there, the initiate may or may not be authorized to receive new hierarchical degrees in the cult.

This relationship is built over time, through what we call *mediumistic development,* and is necessarily linked to initiation and rites of passage. Sidnei Barreto Nogueira, who has a Ph.D. in linguistics, describes the initiation rites of Candomblé, one of the variations of African practices found in present-day Brazil. These rites are also valid for all other variations of African Brazilian religious practices.

> It is a set of sacred rites of African origin that intend to put man in line with his choice in Orun [Heaven]—a parallel universe to Aye [Earth]. According to the Nago world view, before we were born, we chose our Orí-destiny; paths are drawn, some unchanging, others not; we choose and are chosen by our ancestry the deities that we should worship for a life in harmony—with longevity, children and prosperity. In this way, initiation into a deity—*Orisha, Vodun or Nkisi,* aims to: (1) put us in conjunction with our choices made in Orun; (2) strengthen our identity—Orí; (3) revere our ancestral—

> we are the result of our yesterday, of our ancestry; (4) praise and thank for our existence; (5) strengthen the ties between Aye and Orun; (6) place ourselves in conjunction with ancestral Africa; (7) strengthen the notion of humanity and family; (8) get rid of possible "negative energies"; (9) configure a rebirth, as a person and as a self-divinity; (10) and, above all, configure a life with health, harmony, strength, serenity and understanding; (11) value "being" over "having"; and "having"—power of exchange—must be the result of the initiate's ability to "be"; (12) strengthen the individual's self-esteem, leading him to freedom through the bond he must establish with his self-nature-divinity. (Nogueira, Facebook comment)

Above all, it is necessary to understand that the relationship of intimacy between a human and a deity or spirit is a constant and gradual construction that aims to reconnect us to the sacred and, more importantly, to make us sacred. At the same time, as a founding basis of Afro-religious beliefs, during periods of possession or spiritual embodiment, the initiate in which these energies manifest themselves ceases to be human and becomes the spirit or divinity itself, which is then recognized and revered as such.

A Little Bit of the History of Kimbanda

TO TALK ABOUT AFRICAN-ORIGIN RELIGIONS it is necessary to talk about the history of Brazil and even of Western civilization. This history is one of colonialism, imperialist policies, slavery practices, and, first and foremost, racism and discrimination. Knowing this history is important for really understanding how African cults underwent regional transformations and aesthetic adaptations in Brazil and Central America; after all, to believe that the way they are practiced in these countries is a literal repetition of what is done in Africa would be, at the very least, naive. It is also necessary to know the history of the social and cultural formation of what became Brazil, especially in the first centuries after the arrival of the Portuguese in 1500, who initiated the practice of slavery at that time. So, before we talk about religion, let's talk a bit about the past. . . .

ORIGINS OF AFRICAN RELIGIONS IN BRAZIL

The history of the white domination and colonialism of Brazil is intertwined with the history of the African diaspora and the slave system that was practiced all over the world. While Europe since ancient times has been the cultural center of the West, Africa has been the commercial center: "from there gold and ivory, intellectuality and labor were exported to the whole world that was interconnected by trade routes" (Silveira 2014, 51).

Even when the trade market shifted to Asia in the Middle Ages, the African continent remained an important commerce source.

By the middle of the thirteenth century, Italy had expanded its commerical activities and dominated trade in the Mediterranean and beyond. Inspired by Italy's activities and success, and with the aim of dominating trade or at least eliminating intermediaries, the Portuguese became pioneers in navigation and exploration, establishing a multicontinental trading system and becoming the world's main economic power. According to Silveira (2014), between 1415 and 1510 several commercial warehouses were established on African soil, using slave labor; beginning in 1452, the Roman Catholic Church authorized this practice.

Eurocentric historiography seeks to equate the slavery practiced by tribal blacks with that of imperialist whites in an attempt to legitimize European slaveholding and to share the responsibility and consequences of slavery. But even though slavery already existed in Africa when whites began enslaving blacks, how it was conceived and practiced in Africa was different from what was practiced in Europe and later in the Americas.

> In ancient Atlantic Africa, slavery was domestic or, to be more technical, a "lineage" or "kinship" term. Such a definition implies recognizing that captive labor in these countries only after the arrival of European settlers became commercial, by the establishment of monoculture farms for export. (Del Priore 2004, as quoted in Silveira 2014, 52)

In the European concept of slavery, which extended to Brazil, Africans lost their origin and identity, while in the African concept individuals were not dehumanized; on the contrary, their individuality was recognized. In addition, one must also consider that Africans often participated in the slave trade or collaborated with slave traders to avoid being enslaved themselves (Silveira 2014).

Of the six million Africans who survived oceanic crossings to the

Americas, four million landed in Brazil and were deliberately separated from their original ethnicities and consanguineous families to prevent their social reorganization and possible revolt. This did not, however, prevent blacks from forming a new group, reidentifying themselves by their shared enslavement, skin color, and spiritual practices. Though their religious practices differed among themselves, these practices contained within them common elements of worship to divinized ancestors and the forces of nature. In addition, the reception of these reorganized groups under the aegis of the confraternities and brotherhoods of the Catholic Church at the time contributed to this unification, maintenance, and redefinition of spirituality, now under the syncretized mantle of the Catholic saints.

The first black brotherhood governed by the Catholic Church dates from 1552 in the northeastern state of Pernambuco.

> In the first century of Portuguese colonization in Brazil, the congregations destined for the "blacks" had as their priority the indoctrination of the slaves, but they also adopted an assistance character inherited from the European popular brotherhoods . . . consisted in deconstructing native societies by pursuing traditional models of worship, leadership, marriage, and association as diabolical and superstitious things, and at the same time re-socializing the uprooted native into new patterns. (Silveira 2006, 146)

The process of black organization and reidentification through religion occurred throughout America. It is right to say that the Voodoo of Haiti, the Santeria of Cuba and the Caribbean, the Regla de Palo of the Dominican Republic and Puerto Rico, the cult of Maria Lionza in Venezuela, and the *calundus** of Brazil, which later would evolve into

---

**Calundu* is an African word meaning "grimace" or "ugly face," named after the way the face changes while in spiritual possession and referring to African-derived religious practices in colonial Brazil.

the Bahian Candomblé and Southern Batuque, are essentially the same practice, each adapted to the particular geography, culture, and available resources of each country and region into which they were inserted.

> [This] (re)structuring took place through adaptations, aggregations, and deletions of original elements [from African religious practices] in consequence of the process of epistemological destitution and the reality available to the Negro who lived in his diasporic condition, without physical or expression freedom, in a complete "material and symbolic uprooting . . . being confined to the process of dehumanization through the successive stages of deterritorialization operated by the transatlantic trade." (Silveira 2014, 49)

The black restructurings and reconfigurations that happened to Africans upon arriving in the Americas cannot, however, be regarded solely from a religious aspect.

> When rebuilding the family, completely crushed by the process of slavery, Candomblé lends to Africans and their descendants the possibility of symbolically re-tying the ties of kinship. In addition, blackened by the family dispersed by the traffic, the Negroes found in Candomblé the chance to survive as citizens and as race. (Nóbrega e Echeverria 2006, as quoted in Eugênio 2017, 51)

In Brazil, the distribution and exploitation of African and African-descendant labor and the consequent formation of cultural niches and founding of religious groups were due to three major economic periods (Silveira 2014):

1. The harvesting of brazilwood (*Caesalpinia echinata*) from 1500 to 1530
2. The cultivation of sugarcane on plantations from 1532 until the middle of 1700

3. The mining of gold in Minas Gerais throughout the seventeenth century

This distribution of slave labor and the consequent social reconfigurations gave rise to the various expressions of African-origin religions in the country: Candomblé in Bahia, Nagô or Xangô in Pernambuco, Tambor de Mina in Maranhão, Macumba in Rio de Janeiro, and Batuque in Rio Grande do Sul, among others. We will now explore the unique histories of some of these variations.

CALUNDUS AND BAHIAN CANDOMBLÉS

Until the mid-1500s, Brazilian Natives were the primary source for slave labor. From that time on, African slave labor came to be dominant, and until the end of the 1680s, official slave policy toward blacks was harsh and punitive. From 1688 onward, the Portuguese Crown opted to moderate this policy, especially in response to the establishment of Palmares, a community of escaped slaves in Pernambuco, and the fear of new hostile organizations arising; the Crown was "convinced that only in this way could it gain accommodation among the parties" (Silveira 2006, 159).

However, even if there was more flexibility in the texts of the slave rules, the practice of slavery was somewhat different and continued to be violent. Only after a crackdown by the Portuguese Inquisition to punish the practice of alternative religions in 1735 and "under a new threat of the collapse of the Empire," the Marquis of Pombal undertook, in 1760

> a reformist policy that . . . would lead the Holy Office to a greater tolerance in the judgment of alternative religiosities, when then those accused of practicing idolatries and other "offenses to God" on the periphery of the Empire passed enlightenly to be apologized for their supposed rusticity and lack of discernment. (Silveira 2006, 162)

It is important to note, however, that tolerance does not mean acceptance or release. Domination over the slaves and the maintenance of power through violence continued and was still supported by the state and church, which directed slave owners to act "without vengeance."

In addition to a generally more moderate attitude toward African religious practices, the empire tolerated the existence of small religious groups on the periphery, which had no social or political prestige. Slaves were also guaranteed time off on Sundays to enjoy as desired, during which they openly performed sacred and profane dances and feasts, often relating them to the official dates of Catholic festivities to make them more valid and acceptable to the Portuguese. It is in this context that the first spiritual practices, called *calundus,* appeared. The Angolan researcher Oscar Ribas observed that "they represent souls of people who lived in a remote time, a distance of centuries" (Silveira 2006, 177). To this designation it is important to pay close attention to the object of our study: the origin of these cults as spirit worship, especially Kimbanda, which began as a cult to the souls of family ancestors.

> [I]n practice, the border between the sacred and the profane feast could be quite nebulous, since African life was impregnated with religiosity, and African religiousness impregnated with animated rhythms. (Silveira 2006, 175)

It is not my intention to trace the emergence and evolution of the *calundus,* work Silveira (2006) has already done and on which I base my studies. However, the characteristics of these practices that Silveira describes, with records dating from 1646, are of great interest in demonstrating the principles of African Brazilian religions and adherents' reinterpretations of earlier African religious practices within the context of their enslavement in Brazil and their contact with Amerindian traditions. To fulfill this purpose, to avoid errors of interpretation and also to recognize the excellent work already done by Silveira, I have transcribed some of the descriptions of these cults. The year bracketed at the beginning of each extract refers to the date these rituals were observed and recorded.

[1646] With a large bowl full of water, with many leaves and a rattlesnake, a jaguar's tooth, the witness saw some black women washing in that bowl to ease their ladies' condition. . . . In the bowl with water she also put a seal, with which she made a cross and a circle around, then put some powder on it and moved with a knife and kept making as if it had been on fire and, leaning over the bowl, spoke to it, looking backwards at the Negroes present, in her language. (Mott 2005, as quoted in Silveira 2006, 178)

[1701] The rite began with songs of atabaques, "canzás" and chants in the "language of Angola." Branca danced for a while wearing only a white thong and torso sprayed with pemba powder, until she jumped and fell to the floor, as if fainted, entering into a Mediumistic trance. Branca then rose and spoke in a strange voice, invoking the spirit of her late eldest son, who hesitated to answer, intimidated by the large number of people present; only possessing Branca after a table was arranged with food and aluá. The spirit then ate and drank the offerings and then entered the bush, from whence he brought an herb to heal Felicia's affliction. (Sweet 2003, as quoted in Silveira 2006, 202)

[1720–1740] Songs, chants and dances began until Luzia [Pinta, African born] went into a Mediumistic trance, when she took a "strap that had tightened on her belly" and dressed in various clothes, headdresses of feathers, bells . . . when in trance, Luzia spoke in a language incomprehensible to whites . . . passing to the session of cures and divinations, in which she used herbs, certain powders, "a certain wine drink," and manipulated symbols. . . . Mameto Luiza, besides the angel, had the capacity of being possessed by spirits of different orders, both ancestors and deities. (Silveira 2006, 207–27)

◈◈◈

It is from these various cults, or *calundus,* that the Bahian Candomblé and Southern Batuque originated. Notes about these *calundus* were first documented at a festival that occurred in 1832 at a farm in Bate Folha in the Brazilian state of Bahia, which would then become the famous Candomblé of the Angola tradition. The practices quoted were prohibited by the government and pursued by the police; therefore they were performed mostly in rural areas as a domestic cult to spirits and family deities, often with only one spiritual medium, the responsible *calunduzeiro,* presiding. However, during the period from 1750–1850/90, with urbanization expanding into rural areas, the same rites began to be organized and practiced in the suburban areas of parishes or in other intermediary spaces, such as between urban centers and large rural farms. It was precisely this "migration" that initiated the substitution of the name *calundu* for *Candomblé.* While they essentially refer to the same type of spiritual cult, it is the difference between their rural versus urban contexts that differ and make historical documents substitute one term for the other.

Though Candomblé can be defined as an African or African Amerindian religious practice in areas of greater urbanization than those of the *calundus,* its structure and organization are derived from them. Although in theory the *calundus* were limited to domestic cults, in practice they had hierarchies and were able to initiate several faithful at the same time. They had a fixed calendar of celebrations, with attendees paying to participate, which ensured the financial independence of the cult's leader. The Candomblé temples, on the other hand, were only able to consolidate themselves through great influence and social and political protection, since they fulfilled not only "social functions for a poor urban population . . . but also middle and even rich members of the society, who sought them out in moments of desperation [sanitary, mainly]" (Silveira 2006, 243).

We must also consider some important political facts. The 1824 Constitution, while maintaining the Catholic religion as the official religion of the state, permitted the domestic worship of all other religions, and article 179 of the Criminal Code of 1830 prohibited persecution for religious reasons "since it respects that of the State and does not offend public morals." To this we also add the following laws: the Eusébio de Queiroz (1850), the Ventre-Livre (1871), the Sexagenarians (1885), and the Lei Áurea (1888), which together culminated in the abolition of slavery in Brazil.

It is precisely during this period that Candomblé da Barroquinha appears in Bahia. Candomblé da Barroquinha is also known in Portguese as the Terreiro* da Casa Branca do Engenho Velho and by its African names, Ilè Àse Ìyá Nasso Oká or, according to Pierre Verger, Ìyá Omi Àse Àirá Intilè. This is the first Candomblé formally organized between 1788 and 1830 and founded by three African ladies: Ìyá Adetá, Ìyá Akalá, and Ìyá Nassô—described by Verger (1997, 28) as "energetic and voluntary women from Kêto, former freed slaves."

> Among the nago in Bahia, the Ketou nation was particularly important, as a result of the numerous wars which, at the beginning of the nineteenth century, opposed the neighboring kingdoms of Abome and Ketou. They were the ones who created the first Candomblé Temple. (Verger 2012, 33)

The Candomblé da Barroquinha is the origin of the other *mother houses,* as these women-founded temples are called, known to date in Bahia as Ilè Ìyá Omin Àse Ìyá Massé, or the Terreiro do Gantois, of the famous Mãe Menininha, founded in 1849; and Ilè Àse Òpó Àfonjá, founded in 1910 and directed until mid-2018 by Mãe Stella de Oxóssi, who passed away in December 2018. Mãe Stella, in addition to her efforts to recognize and maintain African-origin religious traditions, also played a fundamental role in preserving the history and practice of those traditions through writing and encouraging literary production by other Candomblé temples. She also published several works herself and was inducted into the Academia de Letras da Bahia (Academy of Letters of Bahia).

**Terreiro* (Bahia and Southeast Brazil) and *terreira* (Southern Brazil) are the Portuguese terms for an African religious temple.

It's from Mãe Stella that I quote the the worldview that contextualizes the emergence of African Brazilian religions. In the following quote she describes one of the main aspects of African belief, from which it is possible to identify the interrelation between the physical and spiritual worlds.

> Those who succeed in returning to the òrun may visit us as spiritual ancestors. . . . What we call soul, an abstract element, will soon become an ancestor, and depending on your degree of commitment to the Orísa religion, will also become a counselor to those who remain. (Santos 2006, 25–26)

Notwithstanding the importance and validity of all other African-origin religions founded and reproduced in Brazil, we will make a leap in the history and geography of the country, from Bahia to Rio Grande do Sul, so that we can understand the evolution of the black religions in the state in which, a few years in the future, Traditional Kimbanda will be founded.

SOUTHERN BATUQUE

Although the presence of black people in Rio Grande do Sul, the southernmost state in Brazil, has been recorded since 1635, it was only in 1737 that it was officially recognized as a Brazilian state, and after that, it is historically accepted that slave labor was established and consolidated in the region.

Rio Grande, a coastal city in the southeastern region of the state and a commercial hub due to shipping ports, was the first city founded in Rio Grande do Sul and, for that reason, is considered the cradle of the African religion in southern Brazil. From there, the practice extended to Pelotas—a nearby city, recognized as the cultural and artistic center of the time. Only at the end of the nineteenth century did the practice reach Porto Alegre, the current political and commercial capital of the state, which was raised to the status of a parish in 1777. At that time, little more than 30 percent of the population of Porto Alegre was black.

> In 1814, most of the [state's] population was made up of non-whites. . . . However, Pelotas is the most important city of the nineteenth century in Rio Grande do Sul, where the meat market pole was located, with the highest concentration of Africans and descendants, surpassing 60%. (Assumpção 2011, as quoted in Silveira 2014, 64)

Still, according to Silveira (2014, 61): "Rio Grande do Sul was never part of the African traffic. The state has always received this labor for continental routes." The author further states that, unlike in Bahia, Africans brought to the state were mostly of Bantu origin and already identified with the Yoruba belief, "practicing and following its precepts and foundations" (Silveira 2014), demonstrating that *calundus* influenced the formation of African-religious practice in the south of the country.

The reconfigured identity of the early Africans of Rio Grande do Sul, coupled with the poverty they faced, prevented and discouraged their return to their native land to reconstruct religious foundations and traditions. This contrasts with what happened in Bahia, with Ìyá Nasso and her spiritual heir Obatossi making frequent trips to Africa to learn the social and political organization of various religions, which they replicated in Candomblé Terreiro, as Verger (2002) explains.

Batuque is, therefore, the name given to the African-origin religion practiced in Rio Grande do Sul and later taken to other countries of Latin America, such as Argentina and Uruguay, where today it counts a great number of followers. Its practitioners prefer to politely characterize it as a group of united nations or, in Portuguese, *nação,* an allusion to its ethnic and ritualistic subdivisions: Òyó, Jèjè, Nago, Ijèsà—names of Yoruba origin—and Kabinda. It is noteworthy that Kabinda is the only name of Bantu origin, and, of the nations of Batuque, it is the only one that maintains a close relationship to the cult of the souls of deceased strangers or of illustrious personages in its tradition and religious ancestry through the foundations and secrets of four deities: Zambirá, Pandilha, Kàmukà, and Zina. These features made Kabinda unique, and years later the worship of these deities (excluding Kàmukà) would be consolidated in the practice of Kimbanda.

Brown (1994, 32) suggests that Kabinda may be related to Macumba, another African-origin religion that is based in Rio de Janeiro. She writes that "a strong candidate for precursor of 'Macumba' (perhaps even an earlier form of it) is the practice known alternatively by Candomblé de Cambindas." The word *Cambinda* in Portuguese is believed by most scholar-researchers to be a corruption of the African word *Kabinda*. We will explore the origins of Macumba in more depth in the next section.

Because of this Bantu-Yoruba cultural mix and the lack of geographic mobility among those of African descent due to poverty during the nineteenth and twentieth centuries, the Batuque was not widely disseminated or practiced in other Brazilian states, and the relationships of religious kinship and affiliation do not extend far. In general, there is no history or sense of belonging beyond one or two generations, which unfortunately means that Batuque temples are not as old as the century-old Candomblé temples of Bahia.

The power structure within a Batuque temple is absolutely centralized: apart from the main priest—called ***bàbálórìsà*** when a man and ***ìyálórìsà*** when a woman and commonly known as *pai* (father) or *mãe* (mother) *de santo*—there are no hierarchies or positions. The priest possesses all the knowledge and power to practice religion, sometimes performing various roles at the same time, such as those of "sacrificers, initiators, oraculists and counselors" (Silveira 2014). In this way, as a rule, the death of the priest responsible for a given temple implies the extinction of it.

For this reason, it is very difficult to accurately trace the origin and chronological continuation of religion in the state. Some records date back to the late nineteenth and early twentieth centuries: Esà Kujobá—an African born in Ijèsà, a state in an ancient African kingdom that once existed in the region of modern-day Nigeria—initiated novices on Brazilian soil between 1900 and 1910, and therefore, it is assumed that the practice of Batuque dates back to previous years. It is not known when Mãe Emília de Oya Lajá, born of African royalty and deceased in 1930, arrived in Brazil, but she eventually landed in Rio Grande, and she is accepted by the religious community as the founder of Batuque's Òyó nation. African-born Custódio Joaquim de Almeida, also called Prince Custódio, is the founder of Batuque's Jèjè nation, having arrived in Rio Grande in 1899; he moved to Porto Alegre in the year 1901. The historical records do not provide a precise birth date for Waldemar Antônio dos Santos, also known as Waldemar de Sàngó Kàmukà, but he is uniformly considered the founder of the Kabinda nation.

In any case, Batuque has as its fundamental basis the same common points that we find in Candomblé and other expressions of the African religions in relation to the belief practiced in Africa: the worship and reverence of deities called ***òrìsàs,*** the divinized ancestors who have control over the forces of nature (Verger 2002), through animal sacrifices and ritual offerings; and the continuity of the spirit after disincarnating and its possible return to the physical world—not through the Christian Spiritist* concept of reincarnation but through the spirit's temporary materialization by means of the phenomenon of possession and through the spirit's symbolic and spiritual representation in rituals practiced in the **Ìgbàlè** (House of Souls) and the **Ilé Ibo Akú** (House of the Dead). The **Ìgbàlè** is

*Spiritism, also called Kardecism, is a religion or spiritualistic philosophy that was started in the nineteenth century by French educator Hippolyte Léon Denixard Rivail, who went by the pen name Allan Kardec. Spiritists believe that all living things are immortal spirits that reincarnate. Spiritism is practiced worldwide, with the greatest number of adherents in Brazil.

the area in religious temples dedicated to worship of the anonymous dead, and the **Ilé Ibo Akú** is the area in religious temples dedicated to worshipping the honorable dead from one's religious and genetic family.

Almost at the same time as Batuque was being established in Rio Grande do Sul in 1908, Umbanda, the first African Brazilian religion to worship Eshus and Pombagiras and the predecessor of Kimbanda, was founded in Rio de Janeiro.

SOUTHEAST MACUMBA

Although the official appearance of Umbanda occurred at the end of the 1900s, its African influence originated a few years earlier with Macumba tradition in Rio de Janeiro. Established as the political center of colonial Brazil, Rio de Janeiro officially became the political capital of the country in 1822. Rio de Janeiro went on to became the financial and commercial center of Brazil as well, due to the weakening of agricultural production in the northeast and the emergence of large coffee farms there and in São Paulo.

The term *macumba* has an uncertain origin, but it is always pejorative and generally used by members of the upper social classes to designate various religious practices linked to black magic and witchcraft, which are distinct but also express a common cultural plurality that can be defined as "Low Spiritism" (Brown 1994, 21) or, as Roger Bastide writes in his book *The African Religions of Brazil: Toward a Sociology of the Interpenetration of Civilizations* (1960, as quoted in Brown 1994, 26), the "disintegrative" phase of African culture at the hands of modern capitalism.

> The "macumba" of black people in Rio de Janeiro is the least interesting of Afro-Brazilian practices, given its mixing with other cults and adulteration in contact with a complicated and elaborate urban civilization. (Ramos 1939, as quoted in Brown 1994)

The earliest known record of Macumba dates from 1904 and was written by the journalist and poet João do Rio. Rio wrote a series of articles under the title "Religions in Rio" for *Gazeta de Notícias,* a now-defunct Rio de Janeiro newspaper. These reports have since been compiled and published in book form (see Rio 1976; Rio 2015). They are perhaps not only the most disparaging and prejudiced accounts of African Brazilian practices written to date but also possibly the funniest because of the way the author narrates his visits to more than ten different religious practices—especially the impressions and conclusions (both correct and prejudiced) he comes to from his experiences with the black "*babáloxás, babalaôs e iauôs*" and his attempts to learn spells and how to "kill any citizen."

Despite this, these articles by Rio have great historical value because through them we can verify that the practice of Macumba was known, albeit in a veiled way, to Rio de Janeiro's bourgeoisie, who sought it as a magical, effective, and guilt-free method of solving their problems.

Likewise, in Rio's account about a visit to the House of Souls, in which members of the bourgeoisie seek contact with deceased relatives and receive guidance and blessings from the spiritual world, the author describes a worship session very similar to the ones found still today on the island of Itaparica, Bahia, in cults of the African **Bàbá Egun**.

In one of his stories, in answer to Rio's question about whether one of the sorcerers has political protection, Antônio, a young black man who guides Rio during his explorations, replies, "Of course he has! What do you think, Sir? There are important men who are 32nd degrees in Freemasonry and who owe bulging amounts to the *alufás* and *babalaôs*" (Rio 2015, 25). To his transcription of these dialogues, Rio appends these notes:

> It is likely that many people probably do not believe in witches or wizards, but there isn't anyone in Rio whose life had elapsed without visiting the dirty houses swirling with the roguish indolence

> of black men and women. In the end, this morbid attraction is a problem of heredity and psychology. Our ancestors believed in the complicated arsenal of spells from the Middle Ages, in the pomp of a science that led the weird wise to the gallows and the stake. . . . We kept the spells in the background, as the philosopher used to say, yet groveling in fear before the African Spell, the Spell imported with the slaves. (2015, 57)

The presence and interest of the bourgeoisie were, however, not due to their active participation in religious communities. On the contrary, it was a business relationship, with many blacks and their descendants making their living from the bourgeoisie: solving problems through witchcraft was *always linked to the payment of smaller or larger sums of money*. The skin color of the one seeking services determined how much was charged—the lighter the skin, the higher the fee.

This transactional relationship was in direct opposition to Kardecist Spiritism, which was publicly and widely accepted by society at the time. While Macumba's practitioners were composed of the blackest and poorest members of society who made a living through their spiritual practices, Kardecist Spiritism was made up of whites with greater economic power who practiced charity for the less affluent. A few years later, Umbanda would rise as an intermediary between these two contradictory forms of religious practices and power (Brown 1994).

THE FORMATION OF UMBANDA IN BRAZIL

Although Traditional Kimbanda can trace its African influences and origins to the *calundus* in Bahia and Macumba in Rio de Janeiro, it owes its existence to Umbanda. Umbanda heavily influenced not only Kimbanda's religious identity but also its cultural, social, and racial identities.

Zélio Fernandino de Moraes

Born in 1891 in São Gonçalo, a metropolitan region of Rio de Janeiro, Zélio Fernandino de Moraes is considered the founder of Umbanda. In 1908, at the age of seventeen, he was affected by a paralysis that the medicine of the time could not explain or cure. One day he announced, "Tomorrow I will be healed"—and he was.

To understand how this miraculous cure came about, his parents took him to the Kardecist Federation of the State of Rio de Janeiro in Niterói. He was invited to participate in a Kardecist session, and on November 15, he and other members of the group were possessed by spirits who called themselves Brazilian Natives and black slaves. The members of the federation invited these spirits to withdraw from the session, warned of their supposed state of spiritual backwardness. Then followed an intense debate between the leaders of the federation and the spirit that had manifested in Zélio.

Why does the brother speak in these terms, intending that the Federation accepts the manifestation of spirits that, by the culture they had when incarnated, are clearly delayed? Why do you speak thus, if I see that I am now addressing to a Jesuit, and his white robe reflects an aura of light? And what is your name, my brother?

He answers:

If you think that the spirits of blacks and Brazilian Natives are delayed, I must say that tomorrow I will be at the house of this apparatus [the name given to the human body possessed by the spirit] to begin a service in which these blacks and Brazilian Natives can give their message and thus fulfill the mission that the spiritual plan trusted them. It will be a religion that will speak to the humble, symbolizing the equality that must exist between all brothers, incarnated and disincarnated. And if you want to know my name that is this: Chief of the 7 Crossroads [Caboclo das Sete Encruzilhadas],*

**Caboclo* is a Portuguese word for a native spirit in African Brazilian religions. It also refers to someone of mixed indigenous and European ancestry.

because there will be no closed paths for me. (Moraes 1908, as quoted in Figueiredo 2015)

◈◈◈

By the next day, November 16, 1908, at Rua Floriano Peixoto, n. 30, Bairro Neves, in São Gonçalo, Rio de Janeiro, Brazil, at 8:00 p.m. sharp—in the presence of members of the Kardecist Federation; Zélio's relatives, friends, and neighbors; and a crowd of strangers who had received the news from the previous night—the possession by the Caboclo das 7 Encruzilhadas took place.

Here begins a new cult in which the spirits of Ancient Africans, who had been enslaved and who disembodied and find no place of action in the remnants black sects, already distorted and directed almost exclusively to the works of witchcraft, and the native people of our land, will be able to work on the benefits of their incarnated brethren, regardless of color, race, creed or social standing. The practice of charity in the sense of fraternal love will be the main characteristic of this worship, which is based on the Gospel of Jesus, having as supreme master our Lord Christ. (Moraes 1908, as quoted in Figueiredo 2015)

◈◈◈

From there, the Caboclo das 7 Encruzilhadas went on to define the norms that would be applied in its cult, including the customs, clothing, and desired behaviors of its participants. In the same way, he defined the name Umbanda. The group formed was called the Spiritist Tent Our Lady of Mercy, to which, once again, the Caboclo pronounced:

◈◈◈

As Mary welcomes the child in her arms, the tent will welcome those who appeal to it in times of distress, all spirits will be heard, and we will learn from those spirits who know more and teach those who know less and none will turn our backs and we will not say no, for this is the will of the Father. (Moraes 1908, as quoted in Figueiredo 2015)

◈◈◈

Although romanticized, this is the version of the creation of Umbanda commonly accepted to the present day. Diana DeGroat Brown, an American researcher at Columbia University, gives in her book *Umbanda: Religion and Politics in Urban Brazil* a harder analysis of history and, although she acknowledges the facts here already told (she personally met Zélio de Moraes during her field research in Rio de Janeiro), relates the emergence of Umbanda to *a process of political and social breakup, with Umbanda's founders turning against Eurocentric Kardecism,* while having a predilection to the African Brazilian rites of Rio de Janeiro's Macumba.

Though it was founded in 1908, Umbanda didn't reach Rio Grande do Sul until the late 1920s and early 1930s, through Otacílio Charão and Laudelino de Souza Gomes (Leistner 2014). Contrary to the white resistance to the blacks, identified by Brown as a factor in the breakup of Kardecism and adoption of Umbanda in Rio de Janeiro, Umbanda in Rio Grande do Sul faced strong resistance on the part of black *batuqueiros* (the name given to the practitioners of Batuque) who did not accept the Spiritist-Kardecist practices within Umbanda.

Mãe Ieda do Ogum

Born on October 14, 1940, Ieda Maria Viana da Silva married young, at the age of nineteen, in December 1959, and became pregnant immediately. In February 1960, during the traditional Feast of Our Lady of the Navigators, on the banks of the Guaíba River in Porto Alegre, while accompanying the procession she suddenly became ill and fainted.

Attended by doctors who diagnosed her with simple symptoms of pregnancy, Ieda Maria recovered. The fainting spells, however, continued to happen daily, and sometimes more than once a day. Advised by a neighbor, her mother, Laudelina Oliveira Viana—who years later would become Mãe Mosa, a well-known Umbanda priestess from Porto Alegre—took Ieda to a local priestess called Grandma. Upon her arrival, the young Ieda manifested, for the first time, possession by a Caboclo spirit: Cacique Supremo da Montanha (Supreme Chief of the Mountain). Mãe Ieda relates in the YouTube video "Umbanda de Caboclo" (Santos 2010) that "my caboclo arrived with his eyes open, talking and singing. And then Grandma made me nine herbal baths and took me to a temple, which was in that temple where I came to belong."

From then on, she began her religious life with Umbanda under the guidance of Pai Zé Maria. In mid-1962, Mãe Ieda began to be possessed by a spirit called Eshu Rei das 7 Encruzilhadas (Eshu King of the 7 Crossroads).

In the second half of the 1960s, she and her Eshu, already affectionately known as Seo 7, were then *crossed* by the hands of Pai Eliseu of the Ogum—from whom, years before, she also received initiations in the Batuque, becoming the ***ìálórìsà*** responsible for the Ilê Nação Oyó, an African Brazilian religious temple that exists to the present day.

Cacique Supremo da Montanha embodied in Mãe Ieda do Ogum

And then came Seo 7, you see? At that time he didn't speak, he was all crooked, he ate candles, he ate glass, ate I do not know what else. . . . My spirit, my Eshu, he had to be crossed because Seo 7 came very strong. Then I went to another temple that worshiped Eshu, where the leader was Pai Eliseu de Ogum. (Silva 2000, as quoted in Silva 2003)

The term *crossed* is widely used by African-origin religions in Rio Grande do Sul and has a very broad meaning, often only being fully understood by its practitioners and in the specific context in which it is used. In this case, *Seo 7 was crossed with* ***Òrìsà Bará,*** which means that he received a new degree of social and spiritual recognition within the community in which he and Ieda were inserted, albeit not without resistance from the traditionalists of the time.

This historical moment came to be known as the Bará Crossing. From then on, the process of the Eshu cult's independence in relation to Umbanda began and so, too, consequently, did the foundation of Kimbanda as a formal religion, as it is practiced to the present day in Rio Grande do Sul. In the past twenty years Traditional Kimbanda has expanded exponentially throughout Latin America, having representation in southeast Brazil since 2009 through the Kingdom of Eshu 7 Facadas and Pombagira Cigana, the first Traditional Kimbanda temple in Brazil outside of the southern states, chaired by Diego de Oxóssi.

The Independence of Eshu

JUST AS ANY CHANGE TO an established order takes time, the process of founding and recognizing Kimbanda as an independent religion did not happen quickly. About ten years after the Bará Crossing, Mãe Ieda then began a pioneering spiritual practice in the state, promoting hitherto unusual rituals: indoctrinating and developing the embodiment of Eshus and Pombagiras in public sessions intended exclusively for worship of these spirits, without the binding or subordination to other spirits from Umbanda or ***òrìsàs*** from Batuque. Some years earlier, she also began the practice of religious initiation and specific rituals to these spirits' mediums as rites of passage of the new religion being formed.

> It should also be reiterated, based on Ortiz (1978), that in these (Umbanda) contexts, Kimbanda never really shaped a specific religious system, existing only as a cosmological aspect of Umbanda's articulated worldview. In the same perspective, Kimbanda existing until the 1960s in the Gaucho [Southern Brazilian] environment refers to this same symbolic breakdown of the Umbandist cosmos, with no religious temples or systems organized specifically around the Eshus, nor even self-referenced Kimbanda temples. It is only after the insertion of the Crossed-Line, via its timid presence in Umbanda, that the worship of those deities will undergo profound

> changes. It is these changes that will engender a new religious form, which will thereafter be self-referred to as Kimbanda, with its own rites and belief systems, as well as a particular worldview and ethos. (Leistner 2014, 141)

In addition, Mãe Ieda established a new revolutionary practice: for the first time the rituals for embodying Eshus and Pombagiras were carried out on the beach—a place that until then was exclusive to the cult of **Yemaya,** the ***òrìsà*** of salt waters—and works were performed to honor the deities of the sea, including the Eshu's Beach Realm, which we will learn more about later.

It is important to stress the significance of this act: the shore was, until then, considered sacred ground and not appropriate for accepting the presence of "minor" spirits. By that time, Eshus and Pombagiras were subordinates, slaves of the ruling caste, and are therefore not permitted on sacred ground. Although Umbanda and Batuque are African-based religions, it is obvious how the segregation of the spirits imitates the organization and hierarchy of slavery.

> Kimbanda, which will develop from then on, no longer refers to a category of accusation concerning the idea of black magic . . . a negative symbolic domain of the Umbandist cosmos . . . and not even to a religious line subordinate to Umbanda's spiritual categories. Nor will it be a survival of the ancient Southeast Macumbas, although the new religious form bears many similarities to these practices and symbolically rehabilitates them in contemporary society. (Leistner 2014, 142)

Hitherto the practice of Eshu's magic and spirituality was solely and directly linked to Umbanda, in which Eshu assumed the role of servant and guardian. Ieda's Bará Crossing and the "desecration" of the beachfront—which heretofore had been a place of worship exclusively for **Yemaya**—served as a rite of passage for the medium and as a political and symbolic act for *an Eshu social and religious departure* from the accepted spiritual and religious hierarchy that had been practiced until then.

Thus, there was a rupture between two religious groups: those who accepted the independence and liberation of Eshu and those who did not recognize the revolution of Eshu and his followers against the spirit castes of Umbanda. It can therefore be said that Mãe Ieda do Ogum is the forerunner of Kimbanda. As Professor José Carlos Gomes dos Anjos, from the sociology department of the Federal University of Rio Grande do Sul (UFRGS), states in the documentary *Caminhos da Religiosidade Afro-Riograndense* (*Paths of Afro-Riograndense Religiosity*):

> [Traditional] Kimbanda gives another answer. In a way, an answer that singles out marginal and rascals forms and makes it possible to think of the sacredness of the marginal, the shapes of the margins. In fact, what is present there, we could think of as ways of practicing existence and practicing the sacredness of existence. They are a set of practices that have dimensions that are philosophical, have dimensions that are political, have dimensions that are aesthetic, have fundamentally sacred dimensions. What is at stake is sacralizing existence or how existence happens to us as something sacred. (Silva and Santos 2013)

In the 1970s, another revolution happened in African Brazilian religious society when Mãe Ieda held, for the first time, a party dedicated exclusively to Eshu, in public and in the middle of the street. The so-called Crossroad Feast—held to this day at the intersection of Luiz Afonso and João Alfredo Streets in Cidade Baixa (the famous bohemian district of Porto Alegre, where Ieda's temple is located)—attracted crowds to see Eshu. This is how Eshu and the people of Kimbanda made friends and history in southern Brazil. In 2017, their political and social importance were officially recognized by the capital city of Rio Grande do Sul, which designated August 13 as the official Day of Eshu King of 7 Crossroads.

Years later, as public attendance of the festivities increased, Mãe Ieda began the celebration of the gala ball in rented halls, spaces outside the temple and commonly used for "profane" social gatherings, demonstrating once again that Eshu is as close to us as our friends, relatives, and neighbors. On the social and political importance of Kimbanda's formation and its subversive nature, Diana Brown concludes the following from her experience during Kimbanda sessions in Rio de Janeiro:

> Here was the quintessence of all the activities most feared and despised by the Umbandistas: the open flaunting of morality as well as the barbaric and "primitive" rituals—animal sacrifices, the drinking of blood, the uses of toads. In the setting of extreme poverty, which contrasted with the rich mansions below, this constituted an unequivocal symbolic statement of defiance and resentment against the upper classes, the political system, and the Church as causes of oppression. It was a reenactment of the drama of the African sorcerer plotting to destroy his oppressor. . . . In their broader sense, the Eshus seem to assert the power and autonomy of the individual to have and to pursue his/her own self-interests, as against the interests and moral codes established by state, civil society, and the family. (1994, 91)

The gala balls thus became famous events in which the Kimbanda community could be seen in their best attire. In a few years, Mãe Ieda would also begin holding the "Valentine's Cocktail," where Seo 7 and his spiritual court celebrate love and life, extolling human feelings and values such as fraternity, respect, and equality.

KIMBANDA STRANDS

The exercise of faith and religious syncretism in Brazil is as pluralistic as its ethnic background. Similarly, though Eshu is present in the various African Brazilian religious manifestations that exist in Brazil, he varies widely in his expressions, and it becomes impossible to classify all these forms. This plurality, this variegated social context, is also one of Eshu's typical qualities. Wherever he is present in a religious variant, he accepts the imposed doctrine of that religious expression and adapts to its form of worship.

We'll describe only the common strands of African Brazilian religious expression found in Southern Brazil that use the name Kimbanda in their classification—from which Ieda's Traditional Kimbanda practice originated. There are thus three main strands to be seen:

1. Crossed-Line Umbanda
2. Luciferian/Satanic Kimbanda
3. Traditional Kimbanda

Crossed-Line Umbanda

Since its inception in 1908, the original Umbanda practice has been limited to three main spirit castes: Caboclos, Ancient Africans, and Children. Although Eshus were present from the outset, they did not take an active role in public sessions; on the contrary, they were invoked *only at the end of religious meetings, without the presence of consultants and visitors,* for the spiritual cleansing of the temple.

Over the years Eshus' presence in Umbanda temples has changed and gained supporters. This "ascent," however, was not absolute. Although the Eshus have come to manifest in their own sessions and attend the general public, their performance has remained subordinate to the spiritual chief of each of those temples (typically, a Caboclo or Ancient African spirit). Likewise, initiations and rites of passage for mediums working with Eshus were and always are linked to the previous performance of rites destined for these "superior" spirits' castes.

> In Umbanda even the height of the Eshu's Cottage, called "Tronqueira," located in front of the temple, has a specific measure to demonstrate its servant character and its lower position in comparison to Caboclos spirits. In this cottage are placed only a very

> small glass of brandy (cachaça) and a lit cigar, because it is not our practice to give subsidies to these spirits. (Cacique Nei 2013, as quoted in Borba 2013, 8)

Caboclos, Ancient Africans, and Children are then called the *spiritual right wing,* supposedly acting on the positive poles of spirituality. In contrast, the Eshus and other Kimbanda spirits are called the *spiritual left wing,* acting on the negative poles. This hierarchy, combined with the dominant Christian culture and the strong presence of the syncretism of the spirits and ***òrìṣàs*** with the Catholic saints, contributes to the demonization of Eshus to this day and reinforces the veiled practice of institutionalized discrimination and racism since its foundation.

Just as, in the mid-1900s, Kardecism condemned the presence of Caboclos and Ancient Africans in its spiritual sessions, considering them "inferior," Umbanda ended up reproducing this discriminatory process by implicating Eshu and Pombagira as minor spirits, subjugated to the Caboclos and Ancient Africans spirits of each temple, who, in their religious tradition, assume the positions of authority.

Luciferian, or Satanic, Kimbanda

Luciferian Kimbanda has no public historical record of its inception nor religious validation of its practices. It is the expression of the cult of Eshu through syncretism with European traditions such as Satanism and Luciferianism, High Magic, or the Goetian rite, whose deities, called daemons, had their names wrongly translated from geniuses to demons. Goetia, a form of ancient European magic, in turn originates from a manuscript called Grimorium Verum, where seventy-two daemons are identified by their kabbalistic names and hierarchized into hordes and armies.

> *The Grimorium Verum* (Latin for *True Grimoire*) is an 18th-century grimoire [book of magic] attributed to one "Alibeck the Egyptian" of Memphis, who purportedly wrote in 1517. Like many grimoires, it claims a tradition originating with King Solomon.

The grimoire is not a translation of an earlier work, as purported, its original appearing in French or Italian in the mid-18th century, as noted already by A. E. Waite, who discussed the work in his *The Book of Ceremonial Magic* (1911), stating:

> The date specified in the title of the *Grimorium Verum* is undeniably fraudulent; the work belongs to the middle of the eighteenth century, and Memphis is Rome.

One version of the *Grimoire* was included as *The Clavicles of King Solomon: Book 3* in one of the French manuscripts S. L. MacGregor Mathers incorporated in his version of the *Key of Solomon,* but it was omitted from the Key with the following explanation:

> At the end there are some excerpts from the *Grimorium Verum* with the Seals of evil spirits, which, as they do not belong to the *Key of Solomon* proper, I have not given. For the evident classification of the Key is in two books and no more. ("Grimorium Verum," Wikipedia 2020)

Syncretism and the comparison between the Goetian daemons and the Eshus first appeared in Aluízio Fontenelle's book *Eshu,* published in the mid-1950s. In the same work appears for the first time the concept of the Opposite Trinity, an attempt to create an unholy parallel to the Holy Trinity of the Catholic Church through the demonization of the Eshus. In the Opposite Trinity, the Eshu hordes are governed by a "high command" of Lucifer, Béelzebuth, and Aschtaroth—as opposed to the Father, Son, and Holy Spirit. Fontanelle thus formalized *the separation of good and evil as represented by Umbanda and Kimbanda*—Umbanda is good as opposed to the evil black magic of Kimbanda.

This syncretism, which does nothing but render disrespect to all religions of African origin, is then reinforced by José Maria Bittencourt in his book *No Reino dos Exus* (*In the Kingdom of Eshus*). Fontanelle and Bittencourt's points of view were widely accepted by the African Brazilian religious community of the 1950s, especially by the more conservative ones who saw in Umbanda a form of pure and immaculate religious expression, in the image of Allan Kardec's Spiritism. In Bittencourt's words:

> If Kimbanda exists, it is because we distinguish good from evil. How could there be the distinction if there was only one pole? Therefore, Kimbanda is, in short, a necessary evil, as it constitutes the first step of our spiritual elevation. . . .
>
> With tears in my eyes I pray to God and the Spiritual Guides and Protectors for the Kimbanda reader, for his recovery, which will be done slowly, since the dear reader has been reborn now and has much to learn in future generations. (2004, 16–18)

From this, and with the growth and popularization of Traditional Kimbanda, which is covered in more detail later in this book, various denominations of Kimbanda began to appear, each composed of parts from Traditional Kimbanda and parts from several other traditions, forming a patchwork quilt but with one point in common: *syncretism with the daemons and the mythical figures of the Antichrist in the formation of the Opposite Trinity.* Eshu, in turn, is then baptized with kabbalistic names and put back into submission, if not to the Caboclos or ***òrìsàs,*** this time to daemons and deities of European magic.

Interestingly, those currently following this strand of Kimbanda frequently condemn the Christian belief in God and Jesus Christ, as they see Lucifer as having the greater vitality. They seem to forget, however, that it is only possible to admit the existence of Lucifer when one admits the existence of God, since each completes and justifies the other. One should also note a serious conceptual error in the syncretism practiced by these strands: while the Eshus belong to the spiritual plane, thus being spirits who lived, died, and return to Earth through spiritual embodiment, the daemons belong to the mental plane, being part of the egregores formed in the collective unconscious and without physical manifestation of any kind, accessible only through mental projections.

Add to that the João do Rio articles in 1904, in which he writes about visiting groups that are declared Satanists, practitioners of regional variations of the Black Mass, a European rite of perversion and subversion of the traditional preslavery mass, and the sacrifice of lambs—not as a means of redemption to God but in praise of Lucifer and Satan.

> The Devil's religion has always existed among us, more or less. I've found *envoutement* and maleficence in the current Satanists' documental chronicles, prior to the spells of blacks and Pedro I. Europe practiced both Black and White Mass in the seventeenth century. It is natural that some fleeing sorcerer planted the seed of evil worship here. The documents—scattered documents with no concatenation that Dr. Justino showed me now and then—tell about the evocations of Pope Aviano in 1745. (Rio 2015, 243)

If in his wanderings in African practices, as noted earlier, João do Rio is guided by a black man without a surname, simply called Antônio, to Satanic rituals, he is then accompanied by Justino Moura, a white scholar who is keen to show Rio his knowledge of the world and tell him details of his practice, his fulfillment of the devil's pact, and his alliance with death. Ironically, it is this same Justino from whom Rio receives the following tearful confession about magic at this time.

> The magic has waned, defiled by African customs and shaman jumbles. Do you know the curse of hatred, the beeswax doll? . . . There was also the rectangular *envoutement* . . . Today, the sorcerers are black, the fluids of an inferior race destined to a fast dominance. The Satanic curses are flooded with palm oil and *caboclo* herbs. (Rio 2015, 251, 253)

Traditional Kimbanda

Traditional Kimbanda—which developed through dissension with Umbanda and was institutionalized by Mãe Ieda do Ogum in the mid-1960s—is also called Kimbanda of Crossroads and Souls. In it, Eshus are organized into seven realms, each one subdivided into nine dominions corresponding to the various forces of nature:

1. Crossroads Realm
2. Cruise Realm
3. Woods Realm
4. Cemetery Realm
5. Souls Realm
6. Lira's Realm
7. Beach Realm

In addition to the realms described above, Traditional Kimbanda still acknowledges the existence of parallel groups with distinct cults. Gypsies, Tricksters or Rascals, Kimbandists Caboclos and Ancient Africans (different from those worshipped in Umbanda), Country Men, Bahians, and Marines also manifest themselves, even though the latter three groups have little or no expression in the general context.

While animal sacrifice is nonexistent or performed in small amounts in Crossed-Line Umbanda, in Traditional Kimbanda *the offering of animal blood in sacrifice is the basis of the religion,* and the number of animals sacrificed increases according to the evolutionary and hierarchical degree that the religious practitioners hold within the cult and the responsibilities assumed by them toward their community. Sacrifices of birds, goats, pigs, and cattle are commonly offered, often in large quantities and several times a year.

Similarly, it's in Traditional Kimbanda that Eshu is released from slavery and becomes independent. He's no longer subordinate to the Caboclos and Ancient African spirits of Umbanda, to African ***òrìsàs,*** or to European daemons, nor is it mandatory for Eshu's medium to be initiated in any other religious tradition other than Kimbanda itself.

This independence of Eshu does not mean, however, the lack of a *bond between initiator and initiate.* On the contrary, Traditional Kimbanda is, par excellence, an initiatic religion with *various and varied degrees to be achieved by its practitioners.*

With a strong African influence, Traditional Kimbanda is based on secrecy and is no exception to the "you can only give what you once received" rule, perhaps the greatest foundation of all religions of African descent. The theoretical and practical knowledge of its spiritual rules are passed orally from generation to generation, which in turn requires its practitioners to attend the temple and to assist in rituals inherent to worship. The learning and the resulting responsibilities give the practitioner the right to know new secrets and experience the next rites of passage and, in turn, grants him or her new rights and duties within the religion in an eternal cycle of practice and learning, or *religare*—a Greek principle that defines religion as a tool for reconnecting the human with the sacred.

AFRICAN INFLUENCE IN TRADITIONAL KIMBANDA

It is misleading to think that Kimbanda is a spiritualist religion based on the rules of dealing with the spirits as defined by French Kardecism. All African religious groups believe in the continuation of the spirit after death, even though most do not believe in reincarnation. The cult of familiar spirits was practiced in Africa before slavery and crossed the ocean, having its first expressions in Brazilian soil through Bantu ethnic groups that arrived in southern Brazil, in the *calundus* of Bahia, and in other ethnic groups throughout Brazil. These spirits were attributed the faculties of postmortem continuation as well as the ability to influence and interfere in the affairs of the living.

> If one falls ill, some ancestor spirit is supposed to be offended and sent the disease, or, if not, the sick person has been bewitched by some living enemy. In any case, the soothsayer should consult with

> the spirits to know who is responsible for that ill and what the remedy is. (Omotobàtálá 1999, 13)

These spirits, however, lose their individuality over the generations and become part of a larger group—the so-called religious ancestry. In the same way, the spirits of Kimbanda lose their proper names from when they were alive and become part of larger groups identified by spiritual names that are related to their realms or powers, such as *Tranca Ruas* (Lock Streets), *Sete Encruzilhadas* (Seven Crossroads), *Maria Padilha, Sete Saias* (Seven Skirts), and so on. Thus, two spirits manifested at the same time in one place can, without any problem, present themselves under the same name, even though they are by no means the same spirit, just as there may be two or more Johns or Maries in the same room.

Communication with these spirits is carried out by priests—in Africa called ***inyanga*** or ***nganga*** and in Brazil called Kimbanda chiefs—through various forms of oracles or through the phenomenon of spiritual embodiment. In this case, when embodied, the ***ngangas*** *lose their consciousness and personality for a while and the invoked spirit takes over,* "coming back from the dead" to talk, give advice, promote healing, drink, smoke, dance, and, above all, commune with the pleasures of life with their faithful.

Another similar theological and linguistic resemblance between African and Kimbanda rituals is the worship of **Kalunga-Ngombe,** the Lord of Death. The word ***kalunga,*** in the Bantu language—adapted in Portuguese as *calunga*—refers to diverse forms of cemeteries. In addition, spirits are believed to live at the top of sacred hills, the *lomba** of Traditional Kimbanda. The trees of these hills should never be cut down and at their feet are laid objects such as arrows, bones, pieces of iron, and ceramics, marking the place where the bodies of the deceased are buried—a clear resemblance to the settlements and the

**Lomba* is a typical southern Brazilian word that means "hill" and is commonly used in sacred songs and invocations.

omotés. As we'll discuss later in this book, a settlement is the physical representation of a spirit's powers crated in an iron or clay vase, and an omoté is a consecrated hole in the ground that keep the most powerful secrets of Kimbanda practice and where the spirit is symbolically buried.

The use of gunpowder and ritual powders, beverages, flowers, and perfumes also has an African influence, as these objects were part of African culture through contact with Eastern merchants. Likewise, the living and the dead are believed to share space and food, and it is forbidden to touch objects or ingest food offered to the deceased at the risk of entering *the other side*. Because of these beliefs, Kimbanda dictates that food may never be distributed during a spiritual session until the ritual songs of the Cemetery Realm have been sung (Omotobàtálá 1999).

ÒRÌSÀ ESU AND ITS RELATIONSHIP WITH KIMBANDA SPIRITS

Although in Kimbanda the Eshus and Pombagiras are independent and not subordinate, it is important to note that the cult of family spirits, both in its African origin and in its Brazilian reconfiguration, has always been linked to the worship of other deities. Moreover, we must not forget that, when previously incarnated, these spirits themselves had their own religious beliefs and practices. By the way, it is precisely these beliefs and the ancestral bond to the African deities that distinguishes the Eshu of Traditional Kimbanda, also called High Command Eshu, from those Eshus presented in other African Brazilian religious expressions, which will be explained later.

This, however, does not imply that Eshu is limited or restricted in his actions or that he lacks autonomy as head of the cult, nor does it imply that Kimbanda practitioners need to be initiated in any tradition other than Kimbanda/Eshu itself. Since both Umbanda and Kimbanda are, each in their own way, Brazilian reinterpretations of African religions and cults, the Eshu spirit itself is therefore a reinterpretation of **Òrìsà Esu,** called **Òrìsà Bará** in southern Batuque. In fact, rather than a reinterpretation, the Eshu spirit is *the very personification of this* ***òrìsà,*** since, in this case, the power of communication and movement assumes human name, form, and customs.

If we look at the various forms of worship in Africa, we'll see that the same reinterpretation happens among the different nations: in Òyó-Ketu in Yorubaland there is **Òrìsà Esu;** in the Bantu ethnic groups of Congo and Angola there is **Inkisi Aluvaia;** and among the Ewe-Fon from Benin is **Vodun Legba,** or **Elegbara**. Although these three figures differ in the ways they're worshipped, they are directly related to the same forces of nature and to the same powers of the universe: movement, sexuality, communication, and, especially, communication between the physical world and the deities.

Regarding the correlation and syncretism between **Òrìsà Esu** and the Eshu spirit, Pierre Verger writes about his visit to a Bahian religious practitioner, initiated to **Òrìsà Esu** in the Candomblé tradition in 1936, where he has a pleasant surprise.

In the back of his garden, in a little house, was a trident-shaped iron, ***Esu bàbá buya's*** *settlement, and an iron chain as the settlement of Eshu 7 Facadas.* They were in the company of Esu Elegbara and Eshu Mulambinho. Behind the door of the house was Eshu Pavená. (Verger 2012, 132)*

It should also be noted that, until the early years of the twenty-first century, religious temples that strictly and openly practiced Kimbanda were rare if not nonexistent, due to historical and cultural factors. Even in southern Brazil, where the Umbanda-Kimbanda-Batuque separation is quite clear among its adherents, the natural process for a medium is the practice of at least two of these traditions,

---

*During my research, it was an honor to find an early-1930s Verger mention of the cult of a spirit with the same name as mine, Exu 7 Facadas (Eshu 7 Knifes).

albeit at different times. If one is independent of the other, this in turn does not exclude the former and, therefore, does not require abandoning beliefs on either side.

Thus, it is correct to say that even though **Òrìsà Esu**—or any ethnic variation of his name—is not worshipped in Traditional Kimbanda, he is praised as a centralizing force, merging and expressing the power of all spirits and forces acting there. This merging happens especially in temples where more than one tradition is practiced; in some cases, **Legba/Elegbara** is even seen as a mix of both forms, ***òrìsà*** and spirit, and so is worshipped and receives offerings in both traditions.

Another important issue to note is the differentiation of the names of the energies worshipped in the African religions in southern Brazil, which makes it easier to understand whether one is talking about the African ***òrìsà*** or the Kimbanda spirit. While in African religions in Bahia and throughout southeast Brazil, both **Òrìsà Esu** and the spirit Eshu are given the same name, in southern states **Òrìsà Esu** is strictly called Bará, leaving the word Eshu restricted to the spirits, whatever their form of worship. With this, we can also realize that, in addition to the recognition and reaffirmation of African origin and influence in the formation of Kimbanda, the various names of the African deity are, above all, honorary titles in Kimbanda's practice, in view of the Bará Crossing mentioned in the previous chapters and one of the titles by which Ieda's Seo 7 is known in Porto Alegre: the Legbara Eshu.

DIFFERENCES BETWEEN UMBANDA'S AND KIMBANDA'S ESHU

It is not only in the forms of worship, however, that the Eshus of Umbanda and Kimbanda differ. Although of little relevance in the day-to-day temple practices, there is one sensitive issue that separates these two religions and is absolutely significant regarding their initiation and rites of passage: *the ancestral bond.*

Umbanda was founded and continues to this day under the

Kardecist principles of *peace, love, and charity.* Its main purpose, beyond the religious practice itself, is to bring comfort and calm to those who seek its temples. Likewise, the spirits that manifest there, be they Caboclos, Ancient Africans, Eshus, or any others, have as their mission to give their unrestricted attention to whoever seeks them. In addition, the Umbanda spirits, organized in groups called *falanges* (phalanxes), make themselves available to the spiritual plan for the realization and maintenance of divine will. Therefore, there is no direct or specific link between a spirit and a medium except the common goal of evolution: the spirits work for the common good in pursuit of spiritual evolution for themselves and the collective, while the medium puts himself at the disposal of these spirits so that they can use, through the phenomenon of embodiment, the medium's physical body, and by this symbolic donation of his body and the spiritual practice done by the spirits, the medium seeks his own evolution. For this reason, it is common in Umbanda for a medium to "receive" (a term commonly used to designate the spiritual embodiment) spirits of the various phalanxes worshipped by the temple in which he or she operates, often receiving more than one spirit from the same phalanx.

Kimbanda, on the other hand, goes in the opposite direction. Spirits are not seeking spiritual evolution nor do they belong to a generic astral work group like the phalanxes; indeed, they are considered to be already evolved, since it would make no sense to worship an involuted or immature energy. For a Kimbanda practitioner, Eshu has already achieved all the necessary evolution and that is why he is allowed to return to Earth through spiritual embodiment to work primarily for the individual good of his medium.

In addition, the Kimbanda spirits have an ancestral link with the medium. This means that *a certain Eshu only embodies into a certain medium and, therefore, is bonded to that medium as they both share a relationship with the medium's ancestors.* Thus the African practice of a ***nganga*** keeping in touch with family spirits and the divine ancestors of a community, but only after he or she has undergone a religious initiation, is relived and resignified in Kimbanda—highlighting the importance of Kimbanda's initiation rituals as a way to effectively connect the spirit with the medium.

From this bond, the spirit's goal is then to care for and work for the spiritual, personal, and material evolution of the medium to which it is linked, just as a father cares for and works for a son. For this same reason, it is not common for Kimbanda initiates to receive more than one Eshu or Pombagira, except under special circumstances.

Seo 7, spiritually embodied in Ieda de Ogum

ESHU AND THE JUDEO-CHRISTIAN DEVIL

One of the biggest issues when it comes to Kimbanda is *the relationship between the Eshus spirits and the Judeo-Christian devil.* Christian dogma condenses within a single figure, the devil, every possible representation of what is evil, dark, marginal, and dangerous. Following this reasoning, humanity has a daily struggle denying its own nature, pretending not to know that *we are all made of energy.* Spirits encapsulated in a physical body, some of us prefer to believe that somehow, apart from everything else in the universe, we are not made of both light and shadow and that evil—ah, evil!—does not inhabit us but instead pursues us.

They seem to forget that for there to be a "devil," it is necessary to believe in an omnipotent, omnipresent, and omniscient "god," creator of all things and father of Jesus Christ, the redeemer of sins. For those who believe in them, this Christ, this God, and this devil, however, coexists and if one does not exist, the others cannot either. And here's the main point of it all: in Kimbanda—as well as in Candomblé and other religions of African origin, except for Umbanda—*there is neither one nor the other, neither God nor the devil.*

This does not mean, however, that these religions do not believe in a divine force that creates life and regulates the energies of the universe. However, these energies are by no means related to those forces worshipped by Christian believers. These faiths have different geographical and theological origins, and we must definitely make this clear: *none of these African origin religions are Christian religions.*

Beyond all this, it is important to realize that there is, nonetheless, *a symbolic value in the word and mythical figure of the devil.* Each of us has different backgrounds, social circles, emotional profiles, and conduct; we use our own vocabulary and are shaped by the environment in which we live and those with whom we relate. Slang, regional and idiomatic expressions, and even our personal vocabulary depend on and are shaped by this environment, by the culture and study we have had access to, and by a host of other social-educational factors. Eshu is the same way!

Think with me: Eshus are spirits and, therefore, have lived incarnated on earth before manifesting as spirits. It is believed that, for the most part, they had this incarnation between the seventeenth and nineteenth centuries, during which they only learned what was possible given the social context in which they existed. As a result, each of these spirits has experienced a unique world with specific qualities with which they identify, affecting what they see, do, and feel.

In turn, during this historical period, the syncretism between the Christian devil and **Òrìsà Esu** was deeply rooted in society. The images and icons representing evil, pain, and immoral and amoral concepts were consolidated in the collective unconscious of all people in the colonial and imperial eras in Brazil, when the influence of European society on the cultural formation of the country was much stronger and more influential than it is today.

Considering these issues and also considering that not only Kimbanda but all African-religious practices are a form of resistance to racism, Christian domination, and the violence arising from them, religious practitioners chose to present their chief spirit as "the devil" or themselves as "devil worshippers" as a defense. If their attackers fear absolute evil coalesced in the figure of Lucifer-Satan and if religion is the only or greatest force of resistance to which one has access (*remember we're talking about slavery and the early postslavery period*), it is natural and practical for the faithful to use their enemy's icons and symbols of fear as a defense against potential aggressors.

In the same way, regarding the use of words like *hell, fire,* and *devil* in some sacred songs in Kimbanda—one of Eshu's best-known sacred songs tells us that "*to get here, I crossed a sea of fire*"—none of us can say where these spirits are now or where they went after death, much less what those places look like. In this context, *hell, devil,* and similar words lose their theological and literal value and gain symbolic value. A spirit calling itself "the devil" and assuming an "infernal origin" becomes a source of pride, akin to war scars as symbols of victory over past hardships.

Spirit-Deities

KIMBANDA CAN GENERALLY BE DEFINED as the *cult of the Rascals,* the so-called Eshus and Pombagiras. However, in its theology, Traditional Kimbanda goes further and organizes the cosmos hierarchically under the concept of energies being either condensed or expanded. In addition, as a marginal religion, it brings together other classes of spirits that, like Eshus and Pombagiras, are also often left out of society, both physically and spiritually.

ESHU MAIORAL

Eshu Maioral, also called Eshu Mor and Eshu Belzebu, carries within it the balance of the universe. Unlike Eshu spirits, which, as already described, are spirits subject to the phenomenon of embodiment, *Eshu Maioral does not embody in any medium, no matter what!* This is because Eshu Maioral is not a spirit and has no earthly life, nor is this spirit disincarnated. Maioral is much more than that: it is a *cluster of energies, a powerhouse.* Maioral is the magical gathering of the positive and negative poles of the universe; the symbolic marriage between male and female; and the concentration of the five elements of magical nature—earth, fire, water, air, and spirit.

Commonly represented by the image of Baphomet—a goat-headed androgynous creature with female breasts and ox feet—it epitomizes universal balance. The position of the hands, pointing up and down, is a clear reference to the rule common to all religious traditions: *All that is above is also below; on earth as it is in heaven.*

Eliphas Lévi, in his book *The Doctrine and Ritual of High Magic,* described Baphomet and his magical and esoteric symbolism in an exemplary way, as well as drawing pictures of him.

> The goat . . . has the sign of the pentagram on his forehead point upwards, which suffices for it to be a symbol of light; with his two hands he makes the sign of occultism, and points above to the white moon of Chesed and below to the black moon of Geburah. This sign expresses the perfect accord between mercy and justice. One of his arms is feminine, the other is masculine, like Khunrath's androgyne whose attributes we had to unite with our goat, since it is the unique and same symbol. The torch of intelligence which shines between his horns is the magical light of universal equilibrium; it is also the figure of the soul risen above matter, even though it comes from matter, as the flame rises from the torch. The hideous animal head expresses the horror of sin, for which the material agent, solely responsible for it, must forever carry the punishment: because the soul is imperturbable by nature and can only suffer by materializing. The caduceus, which takes the place of the generative organ, represents eternal life; the belly covered in scales is water; the circle which is above is the atmosphere; the feathers which come thereafter are the emblem of the volatile; then humanity is represented by the two breasts and the androgynous arms of the sphinx of the occult sciences.
>
> Thus is the darkness of the infernal sanctuary dissipated, thus is the sphinx of the terrors of the Middle Ages surmised and thrown off his throne; *quomodo cecidisti, Lucifer?* The terrible Baphomet is no more, like all those other monstrous idols, the enigmas of the ancient science and its dreams, it is but an innocent and even pious hieroglyph. (2017, 317–18)

Eliphas Lévi's drawing of Baphomet

Lévi also clarifies that the name Baphomet is the kabbalistic abbreviation of TEM OHP AB, or *Templi omnium hominum pacis abbas,* which means "father of the temple, the universal peace of men." Tata Augustin de Satã, one of Kimbanda's exponents in southeast Brazil in the mid-1970s, describes the hierarchical position of Maioral in a famous Kimbanda sacred song.

Olha a catira da Umbanda,
Espia, espia quem vem lá.

É o chefe, é o Rei da Kimbanda,
Chefe dos chefes, é o Maioral.

Oh worshippers of Umbanda,
Look, look who's coming there.
It's the master, the Kimbanda King,
Chief of all chiefs, it is Maioral.

ESHU AND POMBAGIRA

Eshu and his female counterpart, Pombagira, are the most well-known spirits of all those manifested in African Brazilian religious practices. While all the other spirits are always kept at a certain distance to divinize and sacralize them, Eshu is close and intimate with human beings and even considered by his faithful as *my buddy* (in Portuguese, *compadre*).

The archetype represented by Eshu creates an almost affectionate bond between people and spirit. For outcasts of every kind—marginal in the literal sense of the word, as in those who live on the margins—Eshu and Pombagira represent human nature itself with all its vices and virtues, free from the moral bonds imposed by Western Christian society. They are therefore parents, siblings, and friends to the faithful, as well as reflections of their worshippers, and they can serve as an element of catharsis.

It is precisely for this reason, combined with the *freedom* that Eshu gains within Kimbanda from his insubordination to other spirits, that he maintains and reproduces, when embodied in his mediums, the ways, tastes, and desires of when he was incarnated and can often be easily confused with a living person.

> They are lovers of the night, gambling, balls and parties of all kinds. The carnival, street parties, drinking, smoking and addictions in general attract them. They are curious, restless, sometimes irreverent and proud, haughty, moody, fickle, and easily irritated. They can be kind and understanding, as well as rude and intolerant; of tender

> words or profanity. They fear nothing; they are bold, insightful, cunning, ironic, very interested, always following, however, the laws imposed by Kimbanda's Maioral. (Omotobàtálá 1999, 41)

The Eshu spirit also takes on the characteristics and principles of the ***òrìsàs*** from which it has inherited its name: it is fast, light, cunning, malicious, clever, and often self-interested. From the oral tradition of Candomblé, some phrases that define Eshu are passed down from generation to generation and symbolize its nature: "*Esu can carry [palm] oil in a sieve without spilling the liquid*"; "*Esu killed a bird yesterday with the arrow he loosed today*"; and "*Esu makes the mistake turn right, and the right turn wrong.*"

Also according to Omotobàtálá (1999), the Kimbanda law imposed by Eshu Maioral to the spirits dictates that

> Eshu gives nothing for free; if someone gives you something without asking for anything in return, then you reward them in triple. You can never give good luck to someone unless they serve you before, because you only give what you've received, otherwise you would break the balance in which you find yourself and you could disappear.
>
> You are the communicator between the worlds, and the loss of balance between them would make you a prisoner forever in one of them, and therefore you would cease to be Eshu to become mortal once again.
>
> You will give something only when it overtakes you, and then it will only happen because they have given you before; however, you can decide who to give and how to give for good or evil—according to the balance you need to restore. (41)

Front and Back Eshus

The Eshus in Kimbanda are organized into seven realms, each with nine dominions. These realms, in addition to their place in nature, also have specific places of worship within the physical domains

Ieda's Seo 7 and Diego's Eshu 7 Facadas, embodied

of the temple and can be broadly classified as *front or back*.

This definition is directly related to the distribution of ritual rooms within a temple, be it Kimbanda, Candomblé, Batuque, or otherwise. In them there is an established order for the placement of some energy: **Esu** or Bará and his inseparable brother **Ògún** always stand over the main gate in front, in a clear reference to the proximity to the street. In the same way, Eshus belonging to the Crossroads, Cruises, Lira, and Beach Realms are classified as *front,* and their rituals are performed either in open air, near the main gate, or inside the main hall of the temple.

Likewise, the Eshus belonging to the Woods, Cemetery, and Souls Realms are classified as *back* and have their own ritual room. In this same room, most of the time, the Eshu settlements of a temple's priest and its initiated are maintained, and it is also there that the *omotés* and the Eshu **Ìgbàlè** (House of Souls) are kept. This room, in turn, is located at the back of the property, just as in the Candomblé and Batuque are **Ilè Ibo Akú** and **Òrìsà Ìgbàlè,** places of worship for the souls of their ancestors.

In addition to the division by type of energy or vibratory range, there is also a generalist classification as to the field of action of the Eshus and their realms. Although the separation among each of the seven realms is recognized, in the day-to-day life of a temple the front realms become one and merge into the Crossroads, and the same is true for the back realms, which merge and unify into the Souls—the reason why Traditional Kimbanda is also called Kimbanda of Crossroads and Souls.

The Magic of Number Seven

The number seven, a powerful and magical number, is present in many religions of the world. Considered sacred, perfect, and powerful by Pythagoras, it is the sum of three (the triangle of the spirit) and four (the square of matter). Seven are the capital sins, and seven are the opposite virtues; seven are the colors of the rainbow, and seven are the musical notes.

Similarly, the number seven and all its multiples are considered Eshu magical numbers, as are the dates ending in seven; in particular, the date July 7, since it was on July 7, 1977, that Mãe Ieda of the Ogum made the first goat sacrifice in Uruguay, in honor of the Eshu King who embodied Pai Armando de Oxalá (Armando Ayala), who until then received only small bird sacrifices and worked subordinate to the Umbanda spirits and who, after that, gained his spiritual manumission. Thus, far beyond the conduct of an individual rite of passage, that date represents the commencement of Kimbanda in that country and its extension beyond the borders of Brazil. For this reason, up to the present day, countless temples in Brazil, Argentina, and Uruguay hold on that date great celebrations in praise of Eshu, offering banquets and sacrifices to these spirits, praying for pioneering, prosperity, health, and the achievement of goals.

Also, on April 7, 2012, Mãe Ieda performed the founding rites of the Kingdom of Eshu 7 Facadas and Pombagira Cigana, overseen by Priest Diego de Oxóssi in São Paulo, the first Traditional Kimbanda temple in Brazil outside the southern states, where the cult originated.

GYPSIES AND THE EASTERN PEOPLE

In Kimbanda, the Gypsy People, also called the People of the East, are spirits parallel to the Eshus and should not be confused with the Gypsy Eshus, which belong to the Lira's Realm. The Gypsy People groups include not only spirits connected to ethnic Gypsies (Calón, Calderash, Romaní, etc.) but also all spirits that originate in East Africa, Eastern Europe, and Asia; spirits of the Egyptians, Indians, Arabs, Moroccans, Turks, Ottomans, Lebanese, Greeks, and even Muslims are included in this classification.

Unlike Eshus, these spirits rarely accept animal sacrifices in their rituals and have an aversion to dealing directly with the souls of the deceased or the ancestors, called the ***egun***. They work closely with the elements and seasons of nature, moon phases, crystals, semiprecious stones, perfumes, and culinary spices. Likewise, it is customary to say that *these spirits are not settled but instead are enchanted or magnetized*—an allusion to their characteristic freedom, their gypsy nature. This interpretation is, however, somewhat controversial and collides with the concept that settlements cause spirits to "stick" or stay in that place, which we consider to be a misinterpretation of the true function of the Eshu settlement and the Gypsy settlement, which I'll explain in the next chapters.

These same spirits can manifest themselves in both Umbanda and Kimbanda without prejudice to their practice. What, in turn, differs between either religion is that, in the case of Kimbanda, the initiation rites of the medium to one of these spirits happens, as already explained, by the family ancestral bond. Thus, not every Kimbanda practitioner may have such a spirit, just as not all people are of Roma or Eastern descent.

Another difference is that in Kimbanda, most of the time, these spirits do not present themselves with their own names but with names related to their spiritual activity: Pandeiro, Estrada, Praia, Violino, Baralho (in English: Tambourine, Roads, Beach, Violin, Deck) are some of them, different from the typically umbandist names taken by these castes—Pablo, Ramiro, Esmeralda, or Sarah, for example.

The Gypsy Eshus and Pombagiras, in turn, are essentially Eshus and follow the same laws as the others, including their proximity to souls and the offering of animal sacrifices. However, they are characterized by having contact and relationship with Gypsy family traditions and natural magic during their previous incarnation.

The altar of Eastern Gypsies at
Eshu 7 Facadas' Kingdom

ZÉ PELINTRA AND THE RASCALS

The Rascal spirits are, par excellence, the expression of Eshu's bohemian and marginal nature, embodied in its greatest representative: the fun and versatile Zé Pelintra. Among the spirits that manifest themselves as Rascals in Kimbanda is the well-known Carioca trickster archetype—a native of Rio de Janeiro who dresses in a white suit, two-tone shoes, and a Panama hat and has a fondness for samba (one could even say a Carioca is born knowing how to dance), *cachaça* (a distilled spirit made from sugarcane) and beer, gambling and small deceits, pub food, and cigarettes instead of traditional cigars.

Charismatic and communicative, easy to befriend and easy to fight, they live to impress men with their bravery and women with their passion; they are eternal lovers. Exponents of the Brazilian way of life, they dance and move with grace and audacity and carry a strong sense of honor and justice in which giving one's word has more value than money.

The Rascals are perhaps the only spirits of Kimbanda that have subdivisions with characteristics more related to the historical and social factors at the time when these spirits were alive than related to their spiritual performance or abilities:

1. Favela Rascals
2. Lapa Rascals
3. Samba Rascals
4. Capoeira Rascals
5. Brave Rascals
6. Piazza Rascals
7. Docks Rascals

Although they all represent aspects of the Carioca trickster, the spirits that are part of this dominion are not necessarily born in Rio de Janeiro, as bohemian culture can be found not just in Rio de Janeiro itself but also in all major urban centers and capitals of Brazil.

Seo 7 Facadas, embodied in Diego de Oxóssi

CABOCLOS AND ANCIENT AFRICANS

In Kimbanda, the spirit castes of the Caboclos and Ancient Africans are also parallel to the Eshus. They are characterized by the spirits of indigenous peoples and black slaves and their descendants who had contact with African American medicine and magic practices. In Umbanda, the Caboclos are mainly identified as the archetype of hunters and keepers of the tribes; in Kimbanda, they are related to sorcery, healing, curandery, and shamans and their rituals.

Caboclo 7 Flechas settlement, at Kingdom of Eshu 7 Facadas

BAHIANS, COUNTRY MEN, AND MARINES

These three archetypes are rarer in Kimbanda than the previous ones. They represent and are related to rural and blue-collar workers, such as sailors, fishermen, dockworkers, cattle ranchers, foremen, and other familiar occupations and social groups from Brazilian history.

Marines differ from the spirits of the Beach Realm for cultural and customs reasons: while in the Beach Realm sea elements such as shells, starfish, and water and sand from the bottom of the sea or from river beaches are used in rituals, for the Marines these elements are forbidden, since sailors believe that having objects belonging to the great waters, taking them from their natural habitat, attracts bad luck.

Originating mostly from undereducated workers, these spirits favor victories over challenges, travel and geographical change, and illicit love and passion, as well as the pursuit of happiness through simplicity. They honor those who have grown through life experience and who, though having little, achieve much and overcome the difficulties of everyday life with a smile on their faces and a friendly word.

Spiritual Hierarchy and Realms

AS WE SAW EARLIER, Kimbanda Eshus are organized into seven realms, an allusion to the tribal and monarchical organization of the African people. Each realm, in turn, is subdivided into nine dominions, corresponding to the various types of places of power, where nature's energy is condensed and can be accessed directly.

It's important to note, however, that this organization and hierarchy does not reflect the ability of individual Eshus and Pombagiras to accomplish magical goals, much less determine which spirits are in charge and which are subordinate. On the contrary, Kimbanda, by establishing boundaries and different fields of action for the deities-spirits, once again stands as a tool for encouraging the faithful to congregate or join together since not even the oldest Eshu acts alone. Furthermore, because where the field of action of one spirit ends the field of action of another immediately begins, a Kimbanda priest can appeal to a variety of spirits through invocations and enchantments.

CROSSROADS REALM

Ruled by Eshu King of 7 Crossroads and Pombagira Queen of 7 Crossroads, the energy point of this realm is at the corners formed by the intersection of two or more roads. Spiritually, these spirits represent and act upon every form of opening and beginning; they are responsible

The symbol of the Crossroads Realm

for breaking free from stagnation and initiating movement toward what is desired, bringing advancement and progress.

They receive their offerings on the street corners of the city. Those who are initiated to an Eshu from this realm as their mentor should always make offerings to him to ensure an open path and to avoid the dangers of the streets.

The Crossroads Realm also provides passage to the other realms of Kimbanda. This is precisely why spiritual sessions always begin with chants of invocation to Eshu Maioral and the Crossroads Realm, which symbolically open the spiritual world. The dominions that are part of this realm and their chiefs are:

Streets Crossroads	Eshu Tranca-Ruas
Lira's Crossroads	Eshu 7 Encruzilhadas
Hills Crossroads	Eshu das Almas
Rails Crossroads	Eshu Marabô
Woods Crossroads	Eshu Tiriri
Cemetery Crossroads	Eshu Veludo
Piazza Crossroads	Eshu Morcego
Space Crossroads	Eshu 7 Gargalhadas
Beach Crossroads	Eshu Mirim

The colors of the Crossroads Realm are red and black, and its symbols are the key and two crossed X-shaped tridents.

CRUISES REALM

Ruled by Eshu King of 7 Cruises and Pombagira Queen of 7 Cruises, this realm has its energy points at all crossings, doors, gates, and on the continuation of a street that follows the Crossroads. These energy points can also be found at the Master Crosses of cemeteries and churches, giant crosses where people light candles and make prayers and offerings, also known as Souls Cruises, which we will discuss later. Spiritually, they represent and act upon passages and points of change and exchange, whether physical, emotional, mental, material, or symbolic. Because they live in doors and gates, these Eshus commonly guard the entrances to religious temples, preventing unwanted energies from entering, especially during spiritual work sessions.

They receive their offerings in the middle of the street or in Souls Cruises, depending on the spirit's magical mysteries. Those who carry an Eshu from this realm as a mentor should always please him by mak-

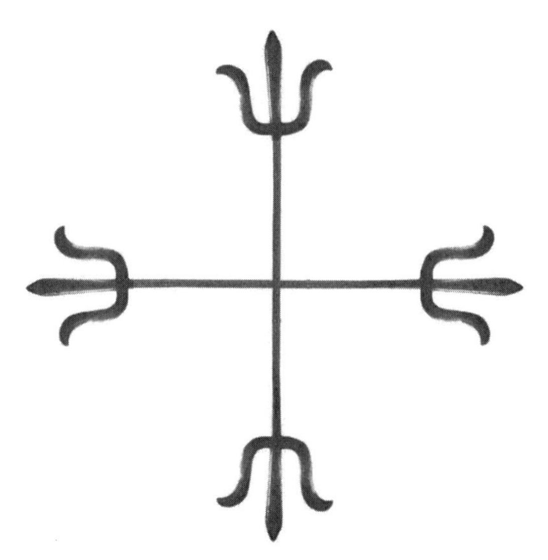

The symbol of the Cruises Realm

ing offerings so that they never stop advancing toward their goals nor abandon their projects and ideals halfway.

If the Crossroads Realm opens up what is desired, it is the Cruises Realm that allows movement and passage from an earlier state to a new one. This is why both are closely linked and often confused. The dominions that are part of this realm and its chiefs are:

Street Cruises	Eshu Tranca Tudo
Piazza Cruises	Eshu Kirombó
Lira's Cruises	Eshu 7 Cruzeiros
Woods Cruises	Eshu Mangueira
Cemetery Cruises	Eshu Kaminaloá
Souls Cruises	Eshu 7 Cruzes
Space Cruises	Eshu 7 Portas
Beach Cruises	Eshu Meia Noite
Ocean Cruises	Eshu Calunga

The colors of the Cruises Realm are red, black, and silver, and its symbol is a two-pointed, cross-shaped trident.

Differences between Crossroads and Street Cruises

The realms of the Crossroads and the Street Cruises are closely linked and are often confused. However, Crossroads and Cruises are different parts of the same place, one becoming an extension of the other; for example, if the Crossroads Realm is the starting point, then Street Cruises is the path taken. The figure on page 62 illustrates this situation in two common cases: an X-shaped street intersection and a T-shaped street intersection.

In addition, it is important to note a historical religious error in differentiating open and closed crossroads as belonging to Eshu and Pombagira, respectively. All the forces of nature maintain in themselves a balance between positive and negative or masculine and feminine

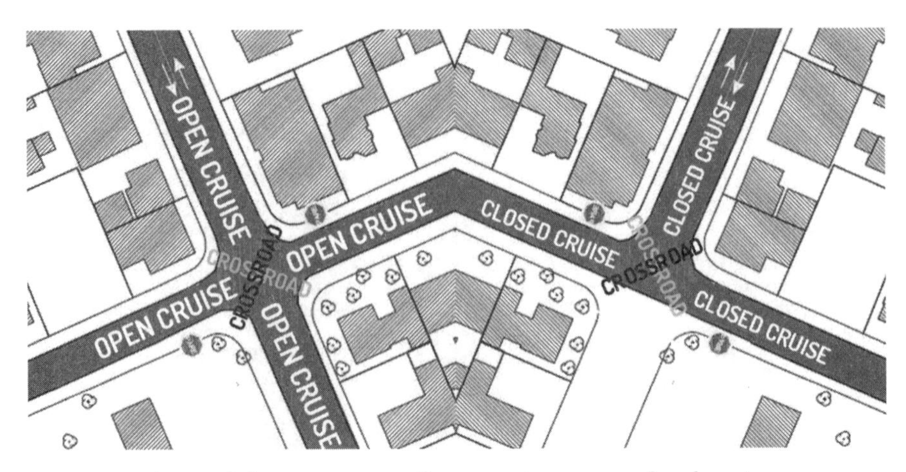

A visual demonstration of open cruises versus closed cruises

energies, which act together, similar to a crossroads. What distinguishes the different types of crossroads and waypoints is not the spirit's gender but the goal to be achieved and the type of energy to be activated. Omotobàtálá (1999) teaches that "the Open Crossroads [X-shaped] is symbolically best used for opening paths, while the Closed Crossing [T-shaped] works the other way around."

WOODS REALM

Ruled by Eshu King of Woods and Pombagira Queen of Woods, the Woods Realm has its energy point in all vegetation sites, fields, hills, and greenery. Spiritually, the ruling spirits represent and act upon the power of plants, earth, and seeds and hence on the cure of disease and the magical utilization of all plant elements.

The spirits that manifest themselves in it are remote and very reserved, with a certain aura of savagery and mystery, characteristic of those who inhabit the depths of the forests and do not make themselves known to the world. They carry within them the wisdom that passes through time; therefore, they are invoked for counseling and appeasement.

They receive their offerings in natural places within civilization, such as gardens and city squares, as well in forests and other wild places. Those who carry an Eshu from this realm as a mentor should always please him by making offerings to ensure complete health, tranquillity, and patience in the face of adversity. It is in the Woods Realm that we'll find Kimbanda's Caboclos and Ancient Africans. The dominions that are part of this realm and their chiefs are:

Trees	Eshu Quebra Galho
Parks	Eshu das Sombras
Beach Grove	Eshu das Matas
Meadows	Eshu das Campinas
Hills	Eshu da Serra Negra
Mines	Eshu Sete Pedras
Snakes	Eshu Sete Cobras
Flowers	Eshu do Cheiro
Seeders	Eshu Arranca-Toco

The colors of the Woods Realm are red, black, and green or maroon, and its symbol is a lit torch and a wolf's head.

The symbol of the Woods Realm

CEMETERY REALM

Also called the Calunga Realm, it is governed by Eshu King of Calunga and Pombagira Queen of Calunga and has its energy point specifically within cemeteries. Spiritually, this realm represents and acts upon chronological time, memories, fears, anxieties, and the other side of life. These spirits govern physical death and symbolic death and are invoked for closure and the end of a cycle.

These spirits receive their offerings at the gates, paths, and cemetery tombs. Those who carry an Eshu from this realm as a mentor should always please him by making offerings to protect themselves against negative energies and make clearing and spiritual-strengthening bonds, since these Eshus are the ones who deal directly with demands and discharges, becoming portals for transmuting negativity. The dominions that make up this realm are:

Cemetery Doors	Eshu Porteira
Tombs	Eshu 7 Tumbas
Catacombs	Eshu 7 Catacumbas
Ovens	Eshu Brasa
Skulls	Eshu Caveira
Cemetery Woods	Eshu Calunga
Cemetery Hills	Eshu Corcunda
Pits	Eshu 7 Covas
Darkness	Eshu Capa Preta/Mironga

The color of the Cemetery Realm is black and shades of gray, and its symbols are the skull and the grave crossed by two tridents.

Cemetery Cruises and Crossroads

Just as there are differences between Street Crossroads and Cruises, the *Souls Cruises,* the *Cemetery Cruises,* and the *Cemetery Crossroads* are different from one another. While the first is the gateway between the

The symbol of the Cemetery Realm

worlds of the living and the dead, the Cemetery Cruises and Crossroads are the crossing points between the paths of a cemetery, formed by both its internal streets and the spaces between each tomb. These differentiations are of utmost importance for initiation rites, as well as for the identification of the Eshu through his *zimba,* the *spiritual and magical signature,* and his *curimba,* the *sacred invocation.*

SOULS REALM

Ruled by Eshu King of Souls, also known as Eshu Omolu, and Pombagira Queen of Souls, the energy point for this realm is located on the hills where the dead are buried and in hospitals, funeral chapels, churches, and morgues. Spiritually, they represent and act upon human emotions and feelings of any nature and on the movement of things, especially from the souls of the deceased to their deserving place.

They receive their offerings in high places and also at the doors of churches and gateways of cemeteries. Those who carry an Eshu from this realm as a mentor should always please him by making offerings for good emotional balance and to ward off the dangers of depression and

The symbol of the Souls Realm

anguish, as these Eshus act on the thin line between sanity and madness. The dominions that make up this realm are:

Hill Souls	Eshu 7 Lombas
Captive Souls	Eshu Pemba
Funeral Souls	Eshu Marabá
Hospital Souls	Eshu Curadô
Churches Souls*	Eshu 9 Luzes
Woods Souls	Eshu 7 Montanhas
Cemetery Souls	Eshu Tatá Caveira
Beach Souls	Eshu Giramundo
Eastern Souls	Eshu 7 Poeiras

The colors of the Souls Realm are black, white, and red or purple, and its symbol is a small mound with a cross on top.

Souls Cruises

The Souls Cruises can be found in church towers, on hills, in cemeteries, and at fatal crash sites on streets and roads. As we have seen, the

*Also known as Churches and Temples Souls

Cruises Realm governs all crossing points, whether physical or symbolic, while the Souls Realm governs every soul no matter its origin. In this way, the Souls Cruises aggregates the functions of both realms and, therefore, is the gateway between the physical and spiritual worlds, allowing communication and movement between the two worlds.

LIRA'S REALM

Ruled by Eshu King of the 7 Liras and Pombagira Queen of the Maries or Queen of Candomblé, this realm has its energy point in all bohemian places, such as brothels, bars, cabarets, gambling houses, and sex shops, as well as in squares and large open-air places where people gather. Spiritually, this realm represents and acts upon music and dance and the arts in every form, inspiration and creativity, material wealth and commerce, and especially the pleasures of the flesh and all forms of sexuality. It is within the Lira's Realm that we will find the Rascals and the Gypsy People.

They receive their offerings near parties of all kinds. Those who carry an Eshu from this realm as a mentor should always please him by making offerings to ensure personal growth and financial

The symbol of Lira's Realm

success and to ward off the dangers of body and soul addictions. The dominions that make up this realm are:

Hells	Eshu dos Infernos
Nightclubs	Eshu do Cabaré
Lira	Eshu 7 Liras
Gypsies*	Eshu Cigano
Rascals	Eshu Zé Pelintra
Eastern	Eshu Pagão / Eshu do Oriente
Filth	Eshu Ganga / Eshu do Lixo
Moonlight	Eshu Malé
Wealth	Eshu Chama Dinheiro

The colors of the Lira's Realm are red, black, and gold, and its symbol is two tridents crossed over a lyre.

BEACH REALM

Ruled by Eshu King of 7 Beaches and Pombagira Queen of Beaches, this realm has its energy point in the sands and dunes that border seas and rivers, in quarries and water mines, and everywhere near fresh or salt water. Spiritually, they represent and act on travel, on movements of exchange, on immensity and the unknown, and on life cycles and their ups and downs.

They receive their offerings in the sand and rocks of the water's edge. Those who carry an Eshu from this realm as a mentor should always please him by making offerings for personal and professional stability to avoid the setbacks of fate and dispel the naïveté and fleeting emotions that are typical of these mediums.

If the Crossroads Realm is the one that opens Kimbanda spiritual

*Again, the Gypsies Dominion and Eastern Gypsies are different energies and spirits and have separate cults and traditions.

The symbol of the Beach Realm

sessions, governing the principle of all movement, the Beach Realm is the one that closes this cycle, governing the comings and goings and the laws of eternal return. The dominions that are part of this realm and its chiefs are:

Rivers	Eshu dos Rios
Waterfalls	Eshu das Cachoeiras
Quarries	Eshu da Pedra Preta
Marines	Eshu Marinheiro
Sludge	Eshu do Lodo
Ocean	Eshu Maré*
Bahian	Eshu Baiano
Winds	Eshu dos Ventos
Islands	Eshu do Coco

The realm's colors are red, black and blue, and its symbol is two tridents crossed under an anchor crowned by three waves.

*Don't mix up Eshu Maré, which is a Kimbanda spirit, with **Oshumaré,** an African ***òrìsà.***

Initiation and Passage Rites

THE MAIN OBJECTIVE OF INITIATION in Kimbanda is to bond the medium to the spirit with whom he or she will relate during religious practices, establishing a link between the medium and the spirit's ancestry. The initiation also seeks to bond the spirit to the temple community, the religious family where the medium is initiated, until all the stages of his or her religious life are fulfilled or until, at the very least, the medium goes through a rite of passage called *aprontamento* (preparation). In addition to establishing a spiritual connection, initiation also symbolizes rebirth: from then on the initiate is expected to behave honorably and respect the spirit and its associated religious family.

For the spiritual connection to become real, a series of specific baths and rituals are performed, creating a step-by-step bond, from the first day of the medium's arrival at the temple until the last day of activities, which culminate in offering sacrifices to the spirit. Importantly, spiritual embodiment is not a requirement for initiation, given that some mediums have other roles and responsibilities within a temple, like Candomblé's titles of ***ogã*** and ***ekedi,*** hierarchical and honorific titles given to men (***ogã***) and woman (***ekedi***) who don't go into trances or any kind of spiritual embodiment or possession.

Different from most ***òrìsàs*** traditions, initiation rites in Kimbanda do not require withdrawal and isolation from the civil and profane world during the ritual days; on the contrary, it is important, as part of the process, that the novice walks the streets without restrictions because at every corner he or she passes there will be Eshus and Pombagiras lurking who will gradually recognize and protect the new *kimbandeiro* (sorcerer). Although the novice is allowed to walk the streets, during the initiation process, which lasts from three to seven days, the initiate must be present in the temple. During this period, the following rituals should be performed:

1. **Spiritual cleansings** and protections to the novice
2. **Animal sacrifices honoring E̱su or Bará,** in case the temple also worships ***òrìsàs***
3. **The Souls Feast,** in which ritual foods and animal sacrifices are offered in honor of the novice's ancestry and to ***eguns***
4. **The Realms Feast,** in which ritual foods and animal sacrifices are offered in honor of each one of Eshu's Realms
5. **Pemba crossing** and *zimbas* signing, in which symbols of power are traced in preparation for the initiation
6. **Eshu's and Pombagira's animal sacrifices,** during which all rites necessary for bonding the spirit with the novice are done

During these rituals, a set of artifacts is consecrated: three strands of beads in the traditional colors of the temple, a sculpture representing the spirit, and a *quartinha,* a kind of water jar or clay bottle representing the medium's body being protected by the Eshu or Pombagira. After initiation, the novice must then make offerings and sacrifices to his spirit at least once a year, in a ritual similar to the Armor Baptism described next, to reinforce the bond created between her- or himself and the spirit, gaining and accumulating *ashé,* the spiritual strength of African traditions.

There is no definite time line for novices to achieve hierarchical and spiritual degrees within Kimbanda—such as the *aprontamento* and the right to use ritual knives for spells or to initiate new novices.

The Souls Feast at Kingdom of Eshu 7 Facadas

Authorization to perform such rites is solely and exclusively given by the chief spirit ruling the temple in which the medium was initiated and may happen within a few months or years of the novice's initiation, in accordance with the dedication of the novice and how much and well he or she has evolved and learned Kimbanda secrets.

THE IMPORTANCE OF THE KNIVES

The initiatory path within Kimbanda consists of several stages that will mark the life of the Kimbandist from his or her initiation to the coronation rite, which makes the initiate a full member of the cult. During this period, some stages have greater ritualistic and social importance because they grant rights and confer recognition and responsibility, such as rites known as knife *ashé*. Animal sacrifice is a fundamental

The Realms Feast at Kingdom of Eshu 7 Facadas

part of the Kimbanda ritual, and for this reason the consecration of the tool that performs these sacrifices is of paramount importance. Once consecrated, the knife loses its profane character and becomes a magical artifact, charged with spiritual and symbolic strength.

Within all religions of African descent, regardless of their customs and practices, one law is common: *You can only give what you've once received*. Now, how could it be possible, then, to give *ashé* to the medium or to feed the spirit without having the vehicle that propitiates the act—that is, the knife that performs the sacrifice—also full of *ashé*?

Moreover, just as in Candomblé* wherein the razor that initiates the

*Unlike Bahian Candomblé, in Southern Brazilian Batuque there are no rites such as hair shaving or body scarifications during initiation; therefore, bonds of honor and respect between novice and priest are created related to the hand and the knives of those who perform the animal sacrifices.

ìyàwó* gains symbolic power to which the initiate owes respect and loyalty, the *initiation knife* also has symbolic value, since both the medium and the spirit "are born" to Kimbanda at the moment the sacrifices of initiation are performed—more specifically, at the moment when the magical acts of bonding between them are performed.

There is a clear distinction between the various authorizations and *ashés* bestowed on each initiation and passage rite and on the purpose of each magical instrument: the knife that performs sacrifices to the ancestors, or ***egun,*** cannot be the same knife used for sacrifices for the Eshus, because these spirits or energies, though close, are distinct and have distinct purposes. Likewise, the knife used to make sacrifices for practical spell purposes is not prepared the same way, and does not have the same *ashé* in it, as the knife used to initiate a new medium. Thus, in Kimbanda there are four types of knives and *knife rites*—namely:

1. Spell knife
2. Initiation knife
3. Bull knife
4. ***Egun*** knife

RITES OF PASSAGE

Nine different rites of passage mark the religious path for initiates. Some of the rites described next are repeated yearly to enhance and strengthen the bond between medium and spirit; otherwise, some of the described rites are not performed for *every* medium, since not all of them have the *spiritual mission* to command, for example, a new religious temple.

Bird Baptism

The Bird Baptism, also known as Birds Crossing, is a kind of preinitiation that aims to protect the medium and bring him or her closer to the

*****Ìyàwó*** is the African word for a novice in Bahian Candomblé.

spirit to which the medium will be initiated. The performance of this ritual does not bind the medium nor the spirit to a temple or religious family; it is not a requirement for initiation and can be performed at any time. In it, a single strand of beads is consecrated to the medium.

Armor Baptism

In this rite, in addition to the the spirit's sculpture and *quartinhas* (clay bottles), already consecrated in the initiation, new elements will be consecrated and will then be grouped next to the sculpture in a clay or pottery vase. These elements are called weapons: forks and iron spears in specific shapes, with which Eshu will symbolically defend the medium. Unlike initiation, in this rite a "feast" is offered only with the ritual foods of the realm to which the spirit belongs.

Knife Baptism: Spell Craft

It is the first great rite of passage after initiation. In it, besides the feast, which is similar to the one offered in the Armor Baptism, a knife called a *spell knife* or *service knife* is consecrated to the spirit. Thereafter, the

Armor Baptism and spell knives consecrated to Eshu 7 Facadas (2009)

medium and the spirit will be allowed to perform bird sacrifices for magic work, but they are not allowed to initiate new mediums. During this obligation, new "weapons" and elements can be added to the vase where the spirit's symbolic sculpture remains.

Aprontamento

Aprontamento is the second great rite of passage after initiation, when the medium is considered ready (in Portuguese, *pronto* or *aprontado*)—that is, the medium is mature and prepared to have access to the secrets and foundations of religion.

In this rite, the Souls Feast, which consists of sacrifices to the ancestors, and the Realms Feast must be offered, just as in initiation rites, since the spell knife will now be consecrated to be used to sacrifice four-legged animals such as goats and pigs. In addition, the imperial necklace will be consecrated, a seven- or nine-strand bead necklace in the specific colors of the spirit and its realm, representing the hierarchical degree achieved.

During this rite, new "weapons" and elements may be added to the vase where the sculpture of the spirit remains, which then receives its sacrifices in the temple's *omoté*. At the priest's discretion one may, in this rite, also create and enchant the spirit's settlement.

Knife Baptism: Initiation

This passage rite may be performed in conjunction with either the *aprontamento* or the coronation. In it, a new knife of specific use is consecrated for the initiation of new mediums in Kimbanda.

Coronation

The coronation is the most important rite of passage within Kimbanda and is the end of a great cycle of learning and practice. The spirit is now called king or queen within the community to which it's related. This recognition is given when the medium is ready and has or is about to inaugurate his or her own temple, initiating new mediums.

Aprontamento and initiation knives (2011)

The word *coronation* comes from the concept that Eshu is king in Kimbanda and, by performing the acts proper to this rite, reigns or commands a new group. For some years now, it has become common in these rites for the Eshu or Pombagira to receive from the hands of the priest a crown that will be worn on feast days thereafter. However, it is not the crown that is the greatest symbol of this rite but the *command scepter*—a kind of cane, the symbol of the highest authority within Kimbanda. Through propitiatory sacrifices, the command scepter is consecrated, and it becomes more than an aesthetic accessory, attaining magical and symbolic properties.

About this, the anthropologist and ***bàbálórìsà*** Rodney de Oxóssi, in his book *The Blessing of the Elderly,* portrays the use of scepters and walking sticks as symbols of power in African-matrix religions, from which we can also infer their value in Kimbanda.

> The walking stick is a symbol of authority, a signal of command and a weapon of peaceful defense. . . . Some carved in noble wood from Africa, full of signs of power, gain the air of scepter, becoming a sign of sovereignty, dignity and legitimacy. The stick denotes that that priest has attained knowledge and is able to impart it. Whoever carries it has reached the apex of social, intellectual, and spiritual hierarchy; is in command and holds the power. (Eugênio 2017, 74)

Through the use of the command scepter, the spirit directs and transmits *ashé* during spiritual sessions, invokes or banishes energies, and causes initiates to go into a trance through a light touch of it on their bodies (Omotobàtàlà 1999). The resemblance between the Kimbanda's command scepter and **Òrìsà Esu**'s ***ogo*** is not superficial or inconsequential. Verger (2012, 127) tells us that "Legba [another name given to **Òrìsà Esu**], among the Fon, is made with a phallus of respectable size. . . . This erect penis is the affirmation of his truculent, violent, shameless character and the desire to shock good manners."

If the medium does not already have his or her own *Eshu Settlement,*

Seo 7, Eshu 7 Facadas and Pombagira Menina at 7 Facadas Coronation Feast, in São Paulo (2014).

it is during this passage rite that the settlement will be created and sacralized. Similarly, if the medium already has a physical space for the new temple, the necessary acts will be performed to consecrate the *omoté* of the chief spirit of that place.

Knife Baptism: Bulls

This rite may be performed jointly with the coronation or in a separate ritual, but only after the creation and enchantment of Eshu's Settlement. In this rite, a new knife to be used specifically to sacrifice bulls, cattle, and buffalo to the spirits is consecrated. A Realms Feast or a specific Spirit's Feast shall also be held at the priest's discretion.

Knife Baptism: Egun

This rite may be performed jointly with the coronation or in separate obligations, but only after the creation and enchantment of Eshu's Settlement. In this rite, a new knife used specifically for sacrifices to the ancestors and for magical works in the Kimbanda's **Ìgbàlè** is consecrated.

For this, the offerings and consecrations of the ritual are performed in the temple's Eshu **Ìgbàlè,** which, although it shares the African name and has a similar ritual function, is not the same as **Òrìsà Ìgbàlè,** even in temples that practice both traditions. During this rite the sacrifices to the spirit may be done as usual. There is also necessarily the Souls Feast and, at the priest's discretion, the Kingdoms Feast. The ***egun*** knife, or ***ìgbàlè*** knife, is devoted only to male mediums or female mediums who do not menstruate.

Liberation or Government Rite

In this rite of passage, the medium and the spirit are then given the right to *govern* themselves, being released from their *priest's knife bonds.* From that moment, the spirit, embodied through the medium, will be allowed to make his own sacrifices, feeding himself and others initiated by him. Receiving of sacrifices from the hands of the medium's priest becomes optional and much more related to the loyalty built during the years the medium has belonged to the temple's family than to a ritual requirement.

Once again, it is worth noting that *you only give what you've once received*. Therefore, no spirit is liberated without the aid of another spirit liberating him, just as no Eshu is crowned through will alone. There is no way to bypass years of practice and religious rites through inherent intuition. Hierarchical titles are given only to those who have passed through the proper rites of passage, the *pronto* and coronation.

ESHU'S SETTLEMENT

The spirit's settlement, sometimes called *Eshu's* ***Nganga****, Eshu's Kabbalah,* or *Eshu's Abassê* when built for initiated persons, is the physical representation of the spirit. As we have seen, Kimbanda Eshus are organized into realms and dominions and can often belong to more than one of these simultaneously—the so-called crossings. In addition, each particular spirit has his own history, spells, and secrets, and all of this is represented in the settlement, through organic elements or magical symbols.

Just as each spirit is unique, the settlement must be the spirit's faithful representation, and therefore each settlement has different elements, shapes, and ways of creation. For this reason, although initiation in Kimbanda is not a requirement for the creation and enchantment of a settlement (the uninitiated may, at the discretion of a priest, have his or her Eshus or Pombagiras settled), only through the initiation rites and the years of experience of the medium and the spirit within Kimbanda law is it possible to identify the characteristics, secrets, and foundations of a specific spirit.

Therefore, unlike the settlements made for the uninitiated, which are built all at once, the Eshu's **Nganga** is built slowly with every rite of passage to which the medium is submitted adding a new charm or element, culminating in his coronation, the rite that then bestows his full power within the religion and fulfills the settlement magic. Prepared only by a Kimbanda priest, with all rites of passage fulfilled and with a vast knowledge of the peculiarities of each realm, it is there that the spirit receives animal sacrifices, as well as the offerings and drinks of its choice.

It is not the purpose of this book to teach how to settle a spirit or offer a "recipe" for doing this. However, it is important to emphasize the importance of the earth element for the enchantment of Eshu in his settlement. It is from the earth and dust gathered in various places and specific circumstances that Eshu will be "(re)born," just as man has his mythical birth: *from earth we have come, to earth we will return, from dust to dust.*

In addition to these elements of earth and dust, other ingredients are also used by the priest at the time of creating and enchanting the settlement, which thereafter becomes the concentration of the spirit's energies and the effective bond between it and its medium.

Eshu Meia-Noite and Eshu Tranca-Ruas Settlements enchanted by Diego de Oxóssi at Kingdom of Eshu 7 Facadas

Settlement Types

Settlements are, therefore, the physical representation and magical focal point of certain energies. Not only embodying spirits can be settled: some Eshus and other energies and powers can be settled, depending on the purpose of the settlement. Thus, we have several types of settlements, each with different objectives, of which here are some examples:

- Embodying the medium's spirit
- Protecting and guarding an individual

Golden Eshu settled by Diego de Oxóssi to a commercial space in Rio de Janeiro

- Protecting and guarding physical spaces (home, offices, temples, etc.)
- Spiritually defending a person or place
- Bestowing wealth and prosperity to persons, shops, or commercial places
- Channeling and opening the intuition for oracle readings

All these settlements can also be created and enchanted for the uninitiated. An example is the settlement of Golden Eshu, which is not

Golden Eshu settled for the Kingdom of Eshu 7 Facadas

an embodying spirit but a power activated to attract material prosperity and wealth to its owner; a proper Kimbanda priest can create this for anyone.

OMOTÉ: ESHU'S TOMB

Various religions and magic traditions around the world use handfuls of earth of all types and locations, as well as holes dug in the ground, to perform rituals and incantations. Eshu in Kimbanda is no different, and as has been said earlier, earth and dust are essential elements in the consecration of Eshu's settlement. However, much is heard about the *omotés,* or Eshu tombs, but little is understood about what exactly they are.

It is common to find Kimbanda practitioners who exalt that their spirits "are part of the people of the hole" or they "eat in the hole," relating them exclusively to the Eshus belonging to the Cemetery or Souls Realms and attributing to them a certain affinity for the harmful and the obscure. The key point, however, is that Eshu, as we have seen, was alive like us; thus, as is natural for every human being, he died and was therefore buried. This is the mystery of the *omoté:* it is, therefore, a representation of the spirit's grave. That grave, a consecrated hole in the ground, is one of Kimbanda's biggest secrets: the grave is the spirit's sacred field, where it will reside for all eternity, and is the major point of its magical power. In it will be planted the spirit's strength.

Mãe Stella de Oxóssi, in her book *Óssósi*: *The Joy Hunter,* explaining the creation of the world and the life cycle from the perspective of African religions says:

> If it is in the bowels of the earth that inhabits the "great creator," the "mystery of the mysteries," the "great spirit," the "essence of all things," there too must be held all the cults as well as the bodies of the deceased ancestors, for that is where we find all the spirits that one day will be reborn or those who'll simply come to visit us. (Santos 2006, 21)

For this reason, the spirits of all realms may, a priori, be settled in an *omoté* that has different ritualistic forms and ways of consecration, just as the spirits and their settlements do. The only exception is the Beach Realm, since its members are believed to have died in the sea, rivers, or lakes and, not being buried in the conventional way, are therefore not worshipped in an earth hole. Importantly, the Eshu's *omoté does not use human bones in their rituals under any circumstances;* whoever does so is unaware of the whole foundation of *omoté* and all the magic of Eshu in the enchantment of the sacred ground and its relationship with the ancestors—those worshipped in Eshu **Ìgbàlè**.

Moreover, starting from when they are first created, the *omotés* should receive offerings and sacrifices annually, just like the medium's spirits. Once dug, an *omoté* should never be filled in with earth but should be covered with a lid that keeps the spirit isolated from the world and prying eyes. Specific rituals and prayers for opening and closing these lids are performed before and after sacrificial rituals.

Crossroads Realm omoté after goat sacrifices, at the Kingdom of Eshu 7 Facadas

ESHU'S COWRIE SHELLS ORACLE

Oracles and practices of divination and communication with the sacred can be found throughout Africa and, by extension, in African-origin religious practices around the world. In the Congo and Angola in particular, various types of oracles have been identified by scholars and religious practitioners who have been there, each using specific elements for divination, such as horns, animal bones, seeds, miscellaneous shells, ceramic shards, and mirrors. However, none of these objects and methods have been as widespread and accepted as cowrie shells.

Present in Candomblé and Batuque, each religious tradition has different configurations and methods of consulting cowrie shells, using twenty-one, sixteen, or eight shells, as well as different ways to consecrate the shells and to qualify the priest for divination. What is common to all these oracular systems is that they provide a means of communication between the profane and the sacred, a means for identifying the desires of the deities and the rituals to be performed to solve the problems of believers or for believers to obtain grace and reach their goals. In the same way, some Kimbanda temples use their own type of cowrie shell oracle to communicate with the Eshus and other spirits.

There are basically two sets of consecrated cowrie shells in Kimbanda: The first, consisting of four cowrie shells, two males and two females, offers direct communication with the spirit invoked upon consultation. The second, more complex set consists of seven small shells and one large shell, one coin, and the Eshu cowrie imperial necklace—a necklace made of a seven- or fourteen-beaded strand in which all the Kimbanda realms and five other energies worshipped in Kimbanda are identified. This necklace, placed on a table, creates a sacred space that represents life and all its situations, a space where Eshu will manifest his word. The priest throws the shells into the sacred space created within the imperial necklace and then interprets the positions of these shells in relation to the various parts of the necklace; how a shell falls is also significant, whether it lands with the opening facing up or down. The priest makes the necessary interpretations and arrives at sought-for answers. The influence of African Brazilian Batuque tradition in the configuration of this type of oracle is clear: just as the ***òrìsà's*** oracle is performed within the sacred space formed by the ***òrìsà*** cowrie imperial necklace, so is Kimbanda's oracle performed within Eshu's imperial necklace.

However, it is important to note that this practice is not part of the Traditional Kimbanda practiced by Mãe Ieda do Ogum but more often found in temples whose rites, when developed and adapted, were under greater African influence. Furthermore, the Kimbanda oracles' divination method, even though cowrie shells are used, has absolutely

Eshu cowrie imperial necklace and oracle

no relation to the ***òrìsà's*** cowrie shell divination process; nor does the oracles' method have anything to do with the Odu Ifá,* which presents various combinations of cowrie shell positions that represent the signs of **Òrúnmìlà,** the founder and grand priest of Ifá and also an ***òrìsà*** of destiny and wisdom. On the contrary, the way each oracle reads the signs and, especially, the energy that manifests and answers through the oracle are completely different.

Omotobàtálá (2013) has identified a cowrie shell practice in Kimbanda that uses twenty-one shells, of which seventeen are used for divination, which suggests direct and exclusive communication with **Òrìsà Esu** and would require a link between Kimbanda practice and more traditional African practices for the divination's consecration. This form of oracle reinforces the African influence in Kimbanda and the bond between the African **Esu** and Eshu, where the latter becomes the messenger of the former but never subjugated to it.

*The Odu Ifá is the literary corpus of Ifá, a Yoruba religion and system of divination. Sixteen books make up the Odu Ifá, with 256 ***odu,*** or verses, that reference all situations, actions, and consequences in life.

Eshu's Magical Signature

ZIMBAS, ALSO CALLED SCRATCHED SIGNS, are a fundamental part of Eshu's magic. It is through them that the spirit presents itself and tells its history, secrets, and origins. In addition, *zimbas* are true portals of communication between the physical and the spiritual world, serving both as the identification or "signature" of the spirit and as signs representing the forces one wishes to activate at any given moment in magical work. Thus, the same spirit can draw different signs in situations that require one or another type of action. Similarly, in many temples the chief spirit, at the beginning of a spiritual session, traces these symbols near the entrance and exit doors, serving as a catalyst of energies.

Commonly scratched with a *pemba,* a kind of conically shaped limestone chalk, *zimbas* can also be traced with other elements such as gunpowder, plant juice, stones, and so on. The way the symbols are arranged—whether straight or curved, simple or complex, up or down, among other configurations—determines which spirit is represented, what kind of energy is invoked, and the purpose of the symbol.

It is important to remember, however, that even though there are several types of *zimba,* the one a spirit uses to identify itself during the initiation and rites of passage is unique and eternal. The composition and intrepretation of *zimbas* is one of the greatest secrets of Kimbanda, and these zimbas are used during these rituals as proof of the existence of the spirit.

It is also extremely important to point out that although *zimbas* resemble Goetia and kabbalistic magic sigils or drawings, they have nothing in common with the meanings and uses of the latter. Identifying them with these other European and Middle Eastern signs and systems is a misinterpretation of Kimbanda and also of Eshu's inner nature as a Brazilian ancestor who was born and died in Brazil.

The figure below provides some examples of *zimbas*. To preserve

Some examples of the signatures of Eshus

religious secrets and to avoid potential self-suggestion of mediums at the beginning of their spiritual development, I do not identify which *zimba* corresponds to which spirit or the meanings of the symbols the zimbas contain.

MUSIC AS MAGIC

Curimba is the name given to sacred songs and prayers that can act as a magical force through vocal expression. Even in Africa, spoken words were an expression of magic, the ***ofó***—a Yoruba word that literally means "enchantment"—that activates the power of the natural elements for the consecration and performance of rituals. In my book *The Sacred Leaves*, I explain in detail how correctly spoken words serve to awaken the inner powers of each leaf for the consecration and creation of baths and fumigations, stressing the maxim that *words have power*. Eshu's *curimbas* are classified according to their purpose—namely:

- Opening a spiritual session
- Ensuring the temple's security
- Summoning spirits
- Praising spirits
- Activating magic
- Bidding spirits farewell

In the next pages are some well-known Brazilian *curimbas* for each of these purposes, written in their Portuguese common form, including slang and word shortenings that allow the songs to rhyme. I have translated these prayer-songs without trying to make them rhyme in English so that you can understand the true meaning of these chants, as some of the words in them have subliminal and ritual meanings that differ from the usual dictionary definitions.

Spiritual Session Opening

Eu vi passar por aqui,
Era o Exu Rei!
Laroiê, laroiê, laruá . . .
Quem manda na terreira?
É o pai Bará!

I saw him passing by,
It was the Eshu King!
Laroie, laroie, larua . . .
Who rules the temple?
It's Father Bará!

Ai eu não passo na rua,
Ai eu não saio na rua,
Sem cumprimentar o Bará da Rua.

I don't walk on the street,
I don't go out on the street,
Without greeting the Street Bará.

Se é Bará eu não sei,
Se é Exu também não,
Só sei que ele veio de lá,
Para trazer a proteção.
E ele corre toda a gira,
Deixa a gira girar,
Exu Bará vai trabalhar.

If he's Bará, I don't know,
Neither if he's Eshu,
I just know he came from far,
To bring protection to us all.

Oh he runs the session,
Let the session go on,
While Eshu Bará works.

O sino da igrejinha
Faz belém, blém-blom.
Deu meia-noite o galo já cantou,
Seo Tranca-Ruas que é o dono da gira.
Oi corre gira que Ogum mandou.

The little church bell
Make it ding, ding-dong.
It was midnight, the cock has crowed,
Mr. Tranca-Ruas who rules the session.
Oh, run the session, it's an order from Ogun.

Temple's Security

A corôa do Rei é mariô, é mariô!
Exu é da pesada,
A coroa do Rei é mariô

The King's crown is made of ***mariwô***!
Eshu is tough,
The King's crown is made of ***mariwô***!

Tem ladeira no caminho,
Nessa casa tem segurança.
Na porteira tem vigia,
À meia-noite o galo canta!

There is a hill on the way,
This temple is safe.
At the gate there is a guardian,

At midnight the rooster crows!

Tem morador, de certo tem morador.
Na casa em que o galo canta,
De certo tem morador.

There is a dweller, oh certainly there is.
In the temple where the rooster crows,
There is a guardian dweller.

Exu Bára que mora na porteira,
Oh na porteira, à meia-noite.
Bebe marafa que nem água,
Quem é que vai dizer que o Tiriri
Não bebe nada?

Eshu Bára who lives at the gate,
Oh at the gate by midnight.
Drink *cacháça* as if it was water,
Who's to say Tiriri
Doesn't like drink?

Tiriri, Tiriri,
Tu que é tão bom,
Toma conta da porta
E do portão.

Tiriri, Tiriri,
You are so good,
Take care of the door
And the gate of the temple.

Lá na porteira, eu deixei meu sentinela.

Eu deixei Seo Meia-Noite,
Tomando conta da cancela.

At the gate, I left my guardian.
I left Mr. Midnight,
Taking care of the gate.

Spirits Summoning

Eu, eu vi a lua,
Clareando a rua, a rua.
Tinha uma garrafa de marafo
Pro Senhor Bará tomar.
Passou um homem, olhou e viu,
Tirou o chapéu e me cumprimentou.
Será macumba, macumba?
Ou será mandinga de amor?

I saw the moon,
Shining on the street, oh on the street.
There was a bottle of *cacháça*
For Mr. Bará to drink.
A man passed by and looked away,
He took off his hat and greeted me.
Is it a spell to attack?
Or is it a love spell?

Eu vou chamar,
No meio da encruzilhada eu vou chamar,
Numa noite encantada!
Ela, Pombagira Rainha,
A dona da Encruzilhada!

I'll call her,

In the middle of the crossroads I will call her,
In an enchanted night!
She, Queen Pombagira,
The owner of the Crossroads!

Olha que eu vou, eu vou
Eu vou mandar chamar meu Povo.
Lá nas 7 Encruzilhadas,
Sem Exu não se faz nada!

Hear all, I'm going to call
I will call for all my Guardians.
At the 7 Crossroads,
Without Eshu nothing is done!

Das Almas, das Almas,
Quem foi que chamou?
Elupandê meu povo,
O Rei das Almas quem mandou!

From the Souls, oh from Souls,
Who is calling?
Elupandê my people,
The King of Souls who commands it!

Galo cantou na Encruzilhada,
Eu vou chamar Exu no tempo,
Eu vou chamar Sete Facadas!

Rooster sang at the crossroads,
I summon Eshu in open fields,
I'm going to call Mr. Seven Stabs!

Spirits Praising

Olha o meu pai chegou no terreiro,
Olha o meu pai, Ele é Quimbandeiro!

Look, my father arrived at the temple,
Look at my father, he is Kimbandeiro!

Tu era tão pequenino,
Mas para mim tu és o Rei.
Tua coroa é de ouro, Exu!
Tu és o Rei das 7 Encruzilhadas!

You were so little,
But for me you were always King.
Your crown is golden, Eshu!
You are the King of the 7 Crossroads!

Quem é que chegou no terreiro, quem é?
Ele é Tranca Ruas das Almas, ele é!

Who arrived at the temple, who is it?
He's Tranca Ruas das Almas, he is!

Nos quatro cantos do mundo,
Quem gira? É ele!
Ai ele é, ele é, ele é!
Ele gira na Calunga e também com Lucifer!

In the four corners of the world,
Who spins? It's him!
Oh it's him! It's him! It's him!
He works at the Cemetery and at the side of Lucifer!

Caveira, Caveira,
Olha o seu Povo que chegou pra trabalhar.
Portão de ferro, cadeado de madeira,
Na porta da Calunga, quem manda é o Exu Caveira!

Caveira, oh Mr. Caveira,
Look at your people who came to work.
If the gate is made of iron, the padlock is wooden,
At the door of the Cemetery, the boss is Eshu Caveira!

Para chegar aqui
Atravessei um mar de fogo.
Pisei no fogo, o fogo não me queimou.
Pisei na terra, a terra balanceou!

To get here
I crossed a sea of fire.
I stepped on the fire, the fire didn't burn me.
I stepped on the ground, the earth rocked!

Magical Activation

Vou fazer minha oração, rodeia!
Sete Facadas quem me deu.
Minha oração tem mironga, oh nganga,
Meus inimigos não me vencem, não!

I'll say my prayer, spin around!
Seven Stabs who thought of me.
My prayer has strength and power, oh priest,
My enemies don't beat me, no they don't!

Tava dormindo, na beira do mar,
Quando as Almas me chamou pra trabalhar.

Acorda Tranca-Ruas, vem trabalhar!
Inimigo tá invadindo a porteira do curral.
Passa a mão nas suas armas, vem guerrear!
Bota o inimigo pra fora, para nunca mais voltar!

I was sleeping on the edge of the sea,
When Souls called me to work.
Wake up Tranca-Ruas, come to work!
The enemy is invading the corral gate.
Get all your weapons, come to war!
Put the enemy out, so he can never return!

São sete covas, são sete catacumbas
Exu do Lodo vem para levar essa macumba!

There are seven graves, seven catacombs
Sludge Eshu comes to take this spell away!

Kimbanda, minha Kimbanda,
O mundo já te conhece!
Quem mexe com quimbandeiro,
Anoitece, mas não amanhece!

Kimbanda, oh my Kimbanda,
The world already knows you!
Who messes with a kimbandeiro,
Goes to sleeps, but never wakes up!

Sete Facadas girou,
Num congá lá da Bahia,
Veio de longe, desmanchar feitiçaria!
Matou um galo preto,
Em noite de lua cheia.

Encontrou toco de vela
Enterrado na areia.

Seven Stabs spun,
In a temple in Bahia,
He came from afar, to dismantle witchcraft!
Killed a black rooster,
On a full moon night.
Found candle stump
Buried in the sand.

Spirits Farewell

Quem samba fica,
Quem não samba vai embora.
A Kimbanda tá chamando,
Os Exus já vão embora.

Who samba stays,
Who doesn't go away.
Kimbanda is calling,
All Eshus are leaving.

Exu bebeu, Exu curiou,
Exu vai embora,
Que a 'banda lhe chamou.

Eshu drank, Eshu cured,
Eshu leaves,
'Cause the realms are calling.

Agora o Malandro vai subir,
Meu Deus, ele já vai embora!
Conversa de Malandro não tem fim,

Boa noite meu senhor, boa noite minha senhora.

Now is time for the Rascal to go away,
My God, he's leaving!
Trickster's chit-chat never ends,
Good night my lord, good night my lady.

Vá embora Exu,
Não se perca no caminho.
Passa no quintal dos outros,
Só não mexa com o vizinho.

Go away, Eshu,
Don't get lost on the way.
Passes in the backyards of others,
Just don't mess with our neighbors.

Mas ela vai como um beija-flor,
Levando sangue no bico,
Deixando plumas de amor.

Oh she goes like a hummingbird,
Taking blood in the beak,
Leaving plumes of love.

Bibliography

Andrade, H. *3333 Exú y Pomba-Gira: Puntos Cantados y Fiscados.* Vol. 1. Buenos Aires: Editorial 7 Llaves.

Bittencourt, J. M. 2004. *No Reino dos Exus.* 6th ed. Rio de Janeiro, Brazil: Pallas.

Borba, R. 2013. "As diferentes formas de culto da Quimbanda no Rio Grande do Sul." Porto Alegre, Brazil.

Brown, D. D. 1994. *Umbanda: Religion and Politics in Urban Brazil.* New York: Columbia.

Eugênio, R. W. 2017. *A bênção aos mais velhos: Poder e Senioridade nos Terreiros de Candomblé.* Mairiporã, Brazil: Arole Cultural.

Exu Rei das 7 Encruzilhadas. "O Reino." Mãe leda do Ogum. Porto Alegre. (Website.)

Figueiredo, B. L. In Zélio de Moraes. São Gabriel, Brazil. 2013. PDF. Accessed 2015.

Fontenelle, A. 1954. *Exu.* 2nd ed. Rio de Janeiro, Brazil: Aurora.

Ilê Nação Oyó: Mãe Ieda do Ogum. "Mãe Ieda do Ogum." Website. Accessed 2015.

Leistner, R. M. 2014. "Os outsider do além: Um estudo sobre a Kimbanda e outras 'feitiçarias' Afro-gaúchas." Dissertation, doctorate in social sciences. Universidade do Vale do Rio dos Sinos (University of Rio dos Sinos Valley), São Leopoldo, Brazil.

Leite, C. R. S. C. 2015. "Na capital gaúcha viveu um príncipe negro." Portal Geledés.

Lévi, E. 2017. *The Doctrine and Ritual of High Magic.* 2 vols. Translated by John Michael Greer and Mark Anthony Mikituk. New York: TarcherPerigee.

Lima, F. 1993. "Exu Elepô: Elemento de identidade Negro-Africana ou Luso-Afro Brasileira." *Revista da Faeeba* 2.

Omotobàtálá, B. O. 1999. *The Kingdom of Kimbanda*. Montevideo, Uruguay: Lulu.com.

———. 2013. *Kimbanda: Mitos y Secretos*. Montevideo, Uruguay: Lulu.com.

Oxalá, M. P. *O Exu Desvendado*. Viamão, Brazil, 2001. PDF. Accessed 2015.

Oxóssi, D. 2021. *As Folhas Sagradas*. 1st ed. São Paulo, Brazil: Arole Cultural.

Rio, J. 1976. *As Religiões no Rio*. Rio de Janeiro, Brazil: Nova Aguilar. First published 1904. Available through Coleção Biblioteca Manancial, no. 47.

———. 2015. *Religions in Rio*. Bilingual edition. Translated by Ana Lessa-Schmidt. Hanover, CT: New London Librarium. First published 1904.

Santos, M. S. A. 2006. *Ọ̀sọ́si: O Caçador de Alegrias*. Salvador, Brazil: Secretaria da Cultura e Turismo.

Santos, R. D., dir. 2010. "Umbanda de Caboclo." Interview of Mãe Ieda do Ogum. YouTube. 9:56.

Silva, J. F. S. S., and R. D. Santos, dirs. and prods. 2013. *Caminhos da Religiosidade Afro-Riograndense*. 2-part documentary. YouTube. 46:40.

Silva, S. D. 2003. "A Kimbanda de Mãe Ieda: Religião Afro-Gaúcha de Exus e Pombas-gira." Thesis, master in anthropology. Universidade Federal de Pernambuco (Federal University of Pernambuco), Recife, Brazil.

Silva, V. G. 2015. *Exu: O Guadião da Casa do Futuro*. Rio de Janeiro, Brazil: Pallas.

Silveira, H. A. A. 2014. "Não Somos Filhos Sem Pais: História e Teologia do Batuque do Rio Grande do Sul." Thesis, master in theology. Escola Superior de Teologia (School of Theology), São Leopoldo, Brazil.

Silveira, R. 2006. *O Candomblé da Barroquinha*. 2nd ed. Salvador, Brazil: Edições Maianga.

Verger, P. F. 2002. *Orixás: Deuses iorubas na África e no novo mundo*. Translated by Cida Nóbrega. Salvador, Brazil: Corrupio.

———. 2012. *Nota sobre o culto aos Orixás e Voduns na Bahia de Todos os Santos, no Brasil, e na Antiga Costa dos Escravos, na África*. Translated by Carlos Eugênio Marcondes de Moura. São Paulo, Brazil: EDUSP.

Werner, A. 2007. "Doctors, Prophets, and Witches." Chapter 16 in *Myths and Legends of the Bantu*. Sioux Falls, N.Dak.: NuVision.

Index

About the Author

DIEGO DE OXÓSSI is a priest of Kimbanda and a *babalorishá* of Candomblé and has provided guidance for personal and spiritual development throughout the world. For more than twenty years, Oxóssi has been dedicated to researching pagan and African Brazilian religions and has given courses, lectures, and workshops on them—their regional forms of expression and the ways in which their rituals can be integrated with society.

Oxóssi graduated with a degree in management processes from Anhembi Morumbi University and has completed Integral Systemic Coaching at Febracis coaching institution. He is editor in chief of Arole Cultural Publishing House. In 2019, he wrote and published, in Portuguese, the trilogy *As Folhas Sagradas* (*The Sacred Leaves,* to be published in the United States in April 2022). Oxóssi lives in São Paulo, Brazil.